TAKE CHARGE!

" It is your choice every single day

*Jessica —
Take Charge!
Be remarkable!
Dill Susan*

Dearest,

With Love,
Be comfortable!

Bill Orson

CONTENTS

FORWARD	5
LIVE ON PURPOSE WITH A PURPOSE	7
PLAN THE WORK, WORK THE PLAN	13
LEADERSHIP	19
COMMUNICATIONS	25
EMBRACE CHANGE	31
THE INTREPID SPIRIT	35
GO SMALL TO BE BIG	39
THE MAGNIFICENT SEVEN	43
DO NOT FALL IN LOVE WITH YOUR IDEA	51
INTEGRITY	53
YOUR PERSONAL P&L	57
WHAT DOES YOUR SUCCESS LOOK LIKE?	61
THE STRATEGY TO GET YOU THERE	65
POSITIONING YOURSELF	69
FINISH THE DRILL	73
WHAT WE HAVE LEARNED OVER THE YEARS	77
DILL'ISMS	81
ABOUT THE AUTHORS	83
OUR STORY WITH SOME STORIES FROM THE ROAD	87

FORWARD FROM DILL AND SUSAN

We have been boots-on-the-ground working with young adults since 1976 on six continents in over 60 countries. We have trained over 100,000 people during that time. Programs we designed have been implemented on all seven continents in over 198 countries and territories. Yes, we have been blessed. During this long journey we have learned many lessons that we are attempting to share with you. This series of thought-starters is meant as a guide for you to use as you plan for the next chapter in your life. We have found that the principles presented in the following chapters work. We want to take a moment to thank you for taking the time to have a read. It is our hope there will be some passages that make you stop and think: Wow, I can do this!

Also, thanks for allowing us in the second part of this book to archive some of our stories in experiential marketing so our grandchildren one day may get a little glimpse and inspiration from our stories from the road. And you may find some interesting, entertaining, and containing a nugget of knowledge.

Remember, It is your choice...you can add value to every situation you find yourself in today...or you can be a drain and try to extract value from those same situations. It is our prayer that you decide to be remarkable! To be Intrepid Spirits!

Dill and Susan
August 2017

CHAPTER 1

LIVING ON PURPOSE WITH A PURPOSE

> All things be ready, if our minds be so
> *William Shakespeare*

It is a hot August day in South Georgia and classes are ready for the Fall Semester at Abraham Baldwin Agriculture College (ABAC) who are known in sports as the Stallions. The students, mostly freshmen, are eager with excitement and anxiety. This is no longer high school. This is a new phase in the journey of life. The young, eager students have heard about Papa Dill, the Co-Dean of the Stafford School of Business, but minds were wondering "who is this person really?" He enters the room in his normal attire; cowboy boots and jeans - the Stetson is left in the office. "Boom!" he yells out. Half of the students almost fall out of their seats. A professor yelling? That didn't happen in High School. "We are STALLIONS!" he yells. "What is a Stallion they ask?" It is someone with a Purpose. Someone with a Plan. Someone who knows his Core Values. Someone who wants to live the STALLION LIFE.

S *ervant Leader*
T *rustworthy*
A *ccountable*
L *oyal*
L *oving*
I *ntreprid Spirit*
O *n Time and On Budget*
N *avigator of the complex world Self-finishers*

Even if you are not an ABAC Stallion, following the values of STALLIONS is a great compass to a great foundation in a great life.

A compass should guide both your personal life and your business. The compass is your purpose. It directs every decision made by your business and is known to all who work with you. Without a compass to guide your business, you are sitting in open waters without forward motion. For instance, at *ignition* the compass that guided the Driscolls was this: make a positive difference in people's lives. When everyone knows where the compass is pointing, your business can sail smoothly. The Driscolls were working with a Russian vodka company who wanted to do a sampling project in Athens, GA, and they wanted to partner with *ignition* to make it happen. Representatives from the company came to the office to shoot a video to promote the project. They hired a model to star in the promotion. The model the vodka company hired was a popular porn star. A member of the *ignition* team was alarmed by this discovery and called the Driscolls to notify them. When they found out, the partnership was called off. Because the *ignition* team knew the compass pointed toward making a positive difference in people's lives, they could make decisions that reinforced that purpose when it was being challenged. They had the ability and knowledge to stand firm in their belief in the mission. The compass was guiding them.

> Every calling is great when greatly pursued
> *Oliver Wendell Holmes, Jr.*

There are two types of people in the world: Radiators or Drains. It is a person's choice each day to choose to be a radiator (positive influence) or a drain (a cancer, a negative influence). A professor, for example, can approach each day in one of two ways - the Drain - "Oh I have to go teach these students. They really are a pain to deal with. Life is just awful." OR the Radiator - "I'm so excited. I get to teach these students. I can positively impact their lives."

Which is a better way to live? Be the Radiator. Always be a positive influence. Focus on what is true, noble, just, pure, and lovely.

Dill and Susan will never forget the day they wrote their very first business plan for their startup company, *ignition*. They had the knowledge of Dill's past business experience, Susan's knowledge of managing large projects and finances, and they had a dream. They created a financial road map to measure monthly success, but also a mission road map to measure their value-based success. It was about more than the money. It was about purpose. It was about making a positive difference in people's lives: their clients, their vendors, their employees, and their families. Sometimes, money is needed to be able to do good things, so don't lose sight of that aspect of a business - but it should never be the sole purpose. Therefore, you need two roadmaps, the *financial* and the *mission*.

As you develop your purpose, don't listen to the Drains. A senior manager at Coca-Cola asked Dill and Susan sneeringly when they told him their mission, "Who do you think you are, the Baptist Church?" At the time The Coca-Cola Company's mission was to increase shareholder wealth. But look at what their mission is today: "To refresh the world. To inspire moments of optimism and happiness. To create value and make a difference."

> Receive my instruction, not silver,
> And knowledge rather than choice gold;
> For wisdom is better than rubies,
> And all things one may desire cannot be compared with her.
>
> *Proverbs 8:10-11*

FINANCIAL ROAD MAP:
A guide to insure your financial success.

MISSION ROAD MAP:
A guide to insure you are making a positive difference.

Dill and Susan realized early on that good business begins with the mission to make a positive difference in people's lives.

As a purpose is developed, it is important to think about how you are going to communicate that purpose to the company. As Dill and Susan were creating *ignition*, they knew that to be successful they needed a way to communicate *ignition's* core values and purpose to the company's thousands of employees through the years to come. Dill and a friend, Tim Brennan, were sitting around debating on what the rally cry was for a company truly wanting to make a positive difference in people's lives. Out of that conversation, *poise* was born.

All over the world, *ignitors* could recite *poise*; they used this motto as their compass when making decisions for the company.

POISE AND PASSION = PURPOSE

From poise, passion was created as one more step in guiding the *ignition* team on how to conduct business the *ignition* way.

P *oise*
A *ttitude*
S *trategic*
S *ubstance and style*
I *nnovation*
O *n time, on budget*
N *on-stop forward motion*

Dill'ism:
Stay low and keep moving!

What is your compass to guide yourself and your team? Take time to develop your own personal plan with a purpose. *It is your choice to live each day on purpose...with a purpose. We hope you join Team Radiators each day!*

> If you want to be successful, It is just this simple.
> Know what you are doing,
> Love what you are doing,
> Believe in what you are doing!
> *Will Rodgers*

Something to Think About:
What is your compass? What is your purpose?

POISE :
An attitude of confidence that comes from complete honesty.
A belief in what you are doing is good for you and the customer.
Complete trust in the mission.

ATTITUDE:
P6+C3+D3 = Winner
P6: Proper Planning Prevents Piss Poor Performance
C3: Don't condemn, complain or criticize
D3: Desire, Dedication, and Discipline

STRATEGIC:
Be strategic in all you do

SUBSTANCE & STYLE:
Have your own style, show who you are, and have the proper costume for the proper situations

INNOVATION:
Being capable of embracing change

ON TIME, ON BUDGET:
The key to success and building a good reputation.

NON-STOP FORWARD MOTION:
Remember the 80/20 rule.
80% of the time things are great,
20% they are bad, but stay low and keep moving.

CHAPTER 2

PLAN THE WORK, WORK THE PLAN

> *No Battle was ever won according to plan...*
> *but no battle was ever won without one*
> *Dwight Eisenhower*

Think about D-Day, there was a plan, but from the first action in executing the plan, not much went according to the Plan. But they had a starting point, a position to adjust, attack, and win the battle. Merriam-Webster Dictionary defines a plan as, "a program or method worked out beforehand to accomplish an objective." The plan helps to communicate to the entire team of what is to be accomplished, what is to be expected, what are the rules, what is the road map. If a person, team or organization doesn't have a plan, they will never know if they have arrived or succeeded and accomplished their purpose.

You can always change the plan; as Dill is fondly known for doing quite frequently, but you must have a plan.

> *All things be ready, if our minds be so*
> *William Shakespeare*

To develop a great plan, one must first seek knowledge. Seeking knowledge is hard work; however, it is worth its price in gold. Seeking knowledge is a life-long endeavor. Seeking knowledge will help one "Finish the Drill" for the roadmap to a successful life with purpose.

> "Thought is the wind. Knowledge is the sail.
> Mankind is the vessel"
> *Unknown*

Once Dill and Susan had a purpose to make a positive difference in people's lives, they then needed a plan. They set about planning their mission, their clients, their services, their financial statement, their legal status, their purpose, their work ethic, and their employee management. Then, they worked those plans.

Something to remember is plans can be changed. Circumstances change and opportunities are created that may require a pivot strategy. Dill and Susan would go back to the drawing board, create and adjust the plans, and keep moving forward. Each year, they would review the past year's performance against their plans - what did they do that they thought they would do, what did they not do, and what should they have done, and then create their annual plan for the next year. Too often small business owners think they are too small to plan; a company is never too small to plan. If a company hopes to be sustainable, it's managers must plan, monitor, and readjust if necessary.

> "We cannot help everyone,
> but everyone can help someone"
> *Ronald Reagan*

Focus is key to success. Many young companies want to be everything to everyone. A clear strategic focus is important. While the Driscolls were Deans at the ABAC Stafford School of Business, they wanted to recruit incoming freshman and retain current students. They focused on recruiting top students. This plan works well for coaches and athletes, and can also work for business professionals. But to accomplish it, they must focus on the top most wanted students. In the Driscoll's companies, every year the team knew the plan. This tactic allowed employees to actively participate in the success of the company. Everyone can help, IF there is a plan; that is true even in people's personal lives.

Focus is key, but the attitude used to attain your success is just as important. Are you a Radiator or a Drain? It is a person's choice each day to choose to be a Radiator (positive influence) or a Drain (a negative influence).

Imagine getting a phone call one late night from your best client and friend saying, "I want to run something by you. Coca-Cola is thinking about taking the Olympic Flame around the world. We need a rough plan in place in forty-eight hours to respond to the International Olympic Committee. Dill, what is it going to take?" You now have forty-eight hours to create the plan. Thank goodness you have been working your planning muscle and know how to dig in and find the solution.

> *Dill'ism:*
> **Go small to be big!**

When this happened to Dill, his planning started with a mantra - Go Small to Be Big! In a matter of twenty-four hours, the decision had been made to create a travel squad of twelve people with a planning team of four. The program would be treated like a military operation with a general (Dill) and a small group of lieutenants, sergeants, and even a chaplain. This team planned and executed one of the greatest events by being PRESENT! Every day. It isn't good enough to just show up; a successful planner must be PRESENT!

People couldn't believe that the planning team to travel around the world with the Olympic Flame representing The Coca-Cola Company would take so few people. But remember go small to be big…four-person planning team, twelve-person travel squad, thirty-four countries, thirty-six days, two 747 jets, coordination with over 400 marketing agencies on the ground, forty-five million consumer interactions, and over three billion media impressions around the world.

As you plan, a *test event* is never a bad idea. For the 2004 Global Olympic Torch Relay, the Coca-Cola Torch Relay leaders from around the world convened in Paris. The team created a mock relay for those who had never experienced a Torch Relay so they would know what to expect when the Olympic Flame was welcomed to their city and country. The learnings were tremendous and adjustments were made to the plan. When the team and the Olympic Flame arrived in each market around the World, the execution was flawless and right on plan. Everything was Perfecto!

Looking at your life, whether it's college, business or your personal life, what is your plan? What is your major, what is your minor, what is your career, what is your occupation, what do you want to learn, what do you need to learn, who is your mentor, who is your mentee, what is your financial plan, what is your budget, what or who is your higher power? These questions will help you formulate your plan for life. And remember, it is ok to change the plan...just have a plan, revisit the plan often and keep moving forward.

> "If you only care enough for a result,
> you will almost certainly attain it.
> Only you must then really wish these things,
> and wish them exclusively,
> and not wish at the same time a hundred
> other incompatible things just as strongly
>
> *William James*

This is an exciting time in your life. Whether you are in college, your first job or your second chapter of life, find your passion. In doing so, you can prevent your passion from becoming just money or the collection of money.

TEST EVENT:
A small-scale trial run of an event to work out any issues that may occur in the larger event.

Money as a passion most often becomes a path of destruction and unhappiness. Always strive to look beyond the money and find your true-life passion.

Now is the time to have a sense of urgency about preparing yourself for your future. Learn how to do quality work now so it is natural when you begin your career. Or if you are already in a career, start today focusing on quality with a sense of urgency.

Take the challenge - stop now and write a rough draft of your plan. Good luck!

Something to Think About:
What do you WANT to Study/Learn?
What do you NEED to Study/Learn?

MY PLAN:

VISION:
___
___
___
___

MISSION:
___
___
___
___

STRATEGY:
___
___
___
___

GOALS:
___
___
___
___

CHAPTER 3

LEADERSHIP

> *Before you can lead yourself or others,*
> *you must first learn to follow*
> *Coleman Ruiz*

Over the years the Driscolls have made an observation on a global scale that seems to be true in all cultures and peoples. The best leaders are those that can first be led themselves. You cannot lead anyone until you learn to follow. Then you can learn to lead yourself.

There are many great leaders to learn from. A favorite for Dill is Sir Ernest Shackleton, a polar explorer who reportedly wrote the following ad in search of men to join him on an expedition:

> Men Wanted:
> *For hazardous journey*
> *Small wages*
> *Bitter cold*
> *Long months of darkness*
> *Constant danger*
> *Safe return doubtful*
> *Honor and recognition in case of success*

It is said that hundreds of men responded. He recruited the men that were experienced, shared his vision and enthusiasm for exploration, those who wouldn't flinch at menial tasks, and those that had the expertise he lacked.

The team left for their journey with high hopes and ambitions. Unfortunately, despite their best planning, they became trapped in ice so severely that the ship was finally crushed and sunken. Unbelievably, he and his men survived a twenty-month ordeal of being stranded in the Arctic Ocean. Shackleton's leadership skills ensured the survival of his team. He led with strength, generosity, compassion, humor, and intelligence. *Shackleton's story* teaches us to hire people with experience, hire people that have common values and vision, hire people that are willing to do what it takes, and those that may be smarter than us in areas that are important to success. He also made sure that every man he hired knew exactly what was expected of him. The team knew the mission and exactly their role and accountability.

The inquisitive would ask how did they survive? By Shackleton's leadership skills - he led with strength (physical and mental strength - weekly soccer matches), generosity (he shared the captain's whiskey), compassion (he understood when someone wanted to give up), humor (he constantly spread joy and laughter), and intelligence (he thought through decisions and consequences). Great lessons for all of us.

> Once you learn to follow, then learn to lead yourself.
> Only you can set the height of your bar
> *Dill Driscoll*

There are many traits of a great leader. If a person can only capture a few of those traits and actively cultivate personal growth, true leadership can become accomplished.

SHACKLETON'S WAY:
Lead with: Strength, Humor, Intelligence, Generosity, Compassion

Below is a list of essential leadership qualities that Martin Luther King, Jr., along with others, have shared over the years:

Do not sugarcoat reality - It is easy to not share the good and the bad with your team in an attempt to protect them. But most people deal best knowing the true reality, and a leader will gain trust when he or she is always honest and open.

Engage the heart - "The heart of the matter is a matter of the heart." Look at volunteers for missions, movements, and charities; they are working from the heart, not the head.

Do not accept status quo - If you do, you will fall behind, and eventually die. There must always be forward motion, especially in today's fast-paced world.

Call people to act up to their highest standards - Always expect people's best, not their worst. Set an example of always giving your best and not accepting anything less.

Refuse to settle - Maybe some may deem it hard headed, but if you believe in something, stand up for it. If you know something is wrong, do not settle - stand strong.

Paint a vivid picture of tomorrow - As Shackleton did, paint a picture for the team of what is success, what it looks like, what does it feel like, even what does it taste like.

Create a sense of urgency - Strong leaders rarely rest on their laurels. There is always a sense of something great is going to happen. Things must be done. There are no lazy people on this team.

Create an atmosphere where the truth is heard - Would the Challenger have not been successful if there had been mechanisms for the truth to be heard?

Lead with questions, not answers - Give the answers and most people will just follow along. Ask questions and different perspectives and ideas will be heard.

Engage in dialogue and debate, not coercion - Sharpen the iron with debate. Attack the problem, not the people. Growth happens when people are challenged and pushed to stand behind their theories and beliefs. By embracing the tension instead of trying to mitigate it, a team will be able to produce imaginative and creative results. The key is to embrace diverse thinking, which creates a natural tension.

Conduct autopsies, not blame - Seek for the truth without blame, encourage learning, encourage honesty without the fear of rejection.

Build red alert mechanisms - Systems that turn information into information that cannot be ignored. It is a good idea to use as Dill calls them, Red Alert! terminology, so your team will be better able to discern when information is absolutely essential. Red alerts give your team members the ability to know when information is vital and when actions need to take place.

> If your actions create a legacy that inspires others
> to dream more, learn more, do more and become more,
> then you are an excellent leader
> *Dolly Parton*

Leadership may come more naturally to some people than others. However, even natural leaders need to continue to learn, assess, and grow. Thinking is hard work. Continuing to grow as a leader is continuous daily hard work. No one ever has all the answers and wisdom. Continue always to strive to grow in wisdom until the day you tell this earth good bye.

> The gardener cannot actually 'grow'
> tomatoes, squash, or beans - she can only foster
> an environment in which the plants do so
> *Stanley McChrystal - Retired Four Star General*

A person knows that they are a leader when in the foxhole of life, they are more concerned for others than themselves. A true leader is someone who has persistence and a strong belief in the path to forge.

> Great leaders will absolutely accomplish their objectives. They will take care of each and everyone of their people
>
> *United States Marines*

Something to Think About:
Who is the most inspiring person in your life and why?
Who is the most inspiring Leader in your life and why?
Are they the same people? Why or Why not?

CHAPTER 4

COMMUNICATION

> Remember the words coming from you in any form
> can be hurtful, so choose them wisely
> *Dill Driscoll*

Everything *communicates*: how you walk, how you talk, how you look, how you dress, what your car looks like, your office, your room, your house. Everything. You are a brand, and you can either take control of that brand and what it stands for or you can let others, through perception, shape your brand out of your control.

Dill has always thought about his costume for the day, the occasion, or the event. His costume is jeans, cowboy boots, and a Stetson (cowboy hat). However, there are occasions where he needs to wear a suit, khakis, or even shorts. He is always thinking: what am I communicating to the people I'm interacting with?

> Do your utmost to be totally transparent
> *Dill Driscoll*

COMMUNICATION:

The imparting or interchange of thoughts, opinions or information by speech, writing, or signs - *Merriam-Webster Dictionary*

A bit of wisdom commonly heard at the Driscoll businesses is, "If you are going to ask for a million-dollar order, you need to look like you know how to handle a million dollars." Why would someone entrust you with a million dollars if you looked unorganized, disgruntled, disheveled, and unfocused? Think about the occasion and dress or act in accordance to what you want to communicate.

Effective communication is a signal of strength. When Dill and Susan started *ignition*, other business executives were flabbergasted that they shared on a quarterly basis the real financial situation of the company. They shared with the team the good quarters as well as the bad quarters. The fear was that if you shared the bad quarters with your team, they would get scared and leave. Adversely, it was feared that if you shared the good quarters with your team, they would get greedy and want more.

However, the Driscolls always believed in dealing with POISE - an attitude of confidence, which comes from complete honesty. By being open and honest with their communication, everyone knew how the company was doing. Good communication can erase gossip, politics, and misperceptions that can damage a business and/or reputation.

Honest communication can be a little frightening at times, but it is vital. The Driscolls have taught their children, it is better to be honest and have Poise than to hide the truth from them. Be careful what you ask; the Driscoll children have been known to tell Dill and Susan what maybe they didn't want to hear when they ask questions to their children. But with an environment of Poise it always works out, and as parents we have learned to be careful what we ask at times.

An example of effective communication was the 20 oz. Coca-Cola Contour Bottle commercialization team which Susan led at The Coca-Cola Company. Their success was primarily due to the team's communication routines. The process was very disciplined throughout the entire commercialization of the new beverage package. Without knowing it at the time, the team operated with Poise.

The team collaborated with each other and with external stakeholders to create the Project Charter. This Charter identified the Mission, the time frame for success, and resources required, the potential hurdles to navigate, and the communication processes. Interdependencies were highlighted with detailed timelines covering the key sub-team areas - technical, financial, operations, Bottler relations, marketing, legal and sales. Weekly in-person meetings were held with the sub-team leaders to discuss interdependencies, red alerts, key findings that would affect others, and celebrate the successes. There were no secrets among the team.

> **Honesty is the first chapter in the book of wisdom**
> *Thomas Jefferson*

Each week, Susan delivered key updates to Senior Management with proposed solutions to the team's issues. That one step was one of the most magical successes of the entire project. Most teams in a corporation like Coca-Cola would offer all their issues to Senior Management with no solutions. This generally resulted in total confusion and slowing of progress as Senior Management with topical knowledge begins to dictate solutions that may not be the most effective. When a team presents solutions, Senior Management is better equipped to react to those solutions and add value in a more structured way.

One other wonderful communication tactic the Contour Bottle team had was with one of the Senior Managers at Coca-Cola. He was known throughout the Company as giving lots of orders, when truth is known; he really knew that some of those orders probably were not the best activities to put time on. But normally the middle managers would run off and try to execute every single one of his orders. The Contour Bottle team tried a different approach. The Senior Manager in the monthly meeting would bark his orders; the team would take them down, go back to the team meeting and systematically determine which ones made sense for the project and which ones did not. The team would then report to the manager which ones they assessed made sense for success of the project. They would also acknowledge the orders they recommended to delay or delete and why. Amazingly, he almost always agreed with the team's assessments. This is a key communication lesson: Most people are open to well thought out push back.

Communication is not just verbal. How a message is delivered impacts how the message is received. At times yelling with enthusiasm or passion may be appropriate; however, at other times, that delivery may be more damaging. The same goes for the quiet delivery; sometimes appropriate, other times not. And then there is technology. Though modern technology has added new avenues of communication, it has also caused confusion. Have you ever sent an email or text that was misunderstood by the recipient? Have you ever replied all to an email or text unintentionally? Have you ever hidden behind an email or text to be mean or nasty to someone? These are all real dangers that can kill relationships.

Tools for communication have evolved over time. In the 1920s, society started with the Movie Screen for sending messages to the world. Then the Movie Screen evolved into the Television Screen in the 1950s. From there in the 1980s, the Computer Screen was introduced quickly followed by the Cell Phone Screen. The *Screens* are changing and changing even more rapidly, thus the thought that needs to go into proper communication of key messages is becoming even more complex.

PROGRESSION OF THE FIVE SCREENS:
Movies
Television
Computer
Smart Phone
Human Touch

However, with all this innovative technology, the most important and effective method of communication is human touch, otherwise known as personal interaction. This was the original form of communication and arguably still has the most impact. When Moses was on Mt. Sinai, how did he communicate and spread God's word? Through word of mouth, and a movement was born that has stayed consistent for thousands of years. Next time you need to communicate an important message, think about picking up the phone or going directly to the person. Don't hide behind emails, texts, or other easier forms of communication.

> No movement was ever started
> without the human touch
> *Dill Driscoll*

As you start to communicate, take a deep breath and think, especially when the topic is sensitive, and above all, always keep your integrity. It is all that you have. Once it is lost, your game is over.

Something to Think About:
What three things can you do to improve your communication?

CHAPTER 5

EMBRACE CHANGE

> Occasionally he stumbled over the truth,
> but he always picked himself up and hurried on as if
> nothing had happened
>
> *Winston Churchill*

Change has become one of the most dreaded words, not because of the word itself, but because of its meaning. Things are going to be different. Humans are resistant to change, or most are. Change is good though and not to be feared. Embracing change is like a tree bending in the wind without losing its footing or leaning to gather sunlight from a better angle. Adapting to circumstances is key to the survival of your business.

As Martin Luther King believed, great leaders do not accept the status quo, meaning they embrace change. To not accept the status quo, you must have a bold attitude toward change and you must be willing to make it happen. Legendary football coach Vince Lombardi understood this. He had these great words to say about it:

Our society, at the present time, seems to have sympathy only misfit, the ne'er-do-well, the maladjusted, the criminal, the loser. It is time to stand up for the doer, the achiever, the one who sets out to do something and does it.

The one who recognizes the problems and opportunities at hand, and deals with them, and is successful, and is not worrying about the failings of others. The one who is constantly looking for more to do.

How does a person stay out there? Pay attention to what is really going on in the world, not the surface, not the conventional wisdom. Observe, really observe. When people stick to their principles, they notice the truth, not the politically correct truth, not the status quo. The interesting thing about change is that people think "it" is new, whatever the "it" is. There are no new ideas. There are no new issues. Just different forms of the age-old truths.

> Embracing change means we are constantly seeking knowledge and looking five years ahead
> *Dill Driscoll*

A friend of the Driscoll's, Sergio Zyman, wrote a book called *The End of Marketing as We Know It*. He identified the Zyman Bakers Dozen as the following:

Marketing is a science not an art,
A well-honed strategy is more important than what your ad says,
Everything communicates and what does this mean to consumers,
The rise of consumer democracy and the threat of consumer communism,
Act locally. Think globally.,
Marketing is too important to be left to the Marketing Department,
Ad agencies are fixated on the wrong things,
It is crucial to increase the marketing budget when sales are down,
Mega brands are a terrible idea, but huge brands are a great idea,
It is suicide to base sales projections on previous performance,
You must be focused on profit, not volume for volume sake,
It is sometimes necessary to enter a category just to kill the category,
All marketers must be accountable to shareholders,

Pushing for a change in the way the marketing industry traditionally thinks is what Sergio was trying to do. Think of Madonna. She embraces change. She has reinvented herself numerous times so that she remains relevant to whatever is relevant at the time. Or, for another example, take something as simple as eyeglasses. At one time, people were embarrassed to wear glasses; now they wear glasses as a fashion statement whether they need them or not.

Businesses do this too. Apple is a company that is all about creating what customers want before they even know they want it. Now that is embracing change. Another great business is UPS, a delivery company that now loves logistics. They haven't walked away from their core, delivering packages, but added to their expertise as a service to some of the largest companies in the world.

> I know well what I am fleeing from,
> but not what I am in search of
> *Michel de Montaigne*

Even communities must make changes to stay alive. For instance, small town Aspen, CO went from silver mining town to ski town to year around resort to an internationally known center for thought with the Aspen Institute. It is a town continuing to stay relevant and grow.

Those that have refused to embrace change die. Kodak created the camera and film industry. They didn't recognize and embrace change and are now practically dead. Massey Ferguson didn't invest and now it is all John Deere. Small towns throughout the U.S. have refused to change and to embrace the future. They are all dying and now community leaders are asking, "Is it too late to reinvent ourselves?"

Change is part of life no matter what generation or community in which one lives. The only thing to do to be successful is to embrace it and ride the waves. Be a *Hero* of change.

HERO:
Someone who sees what needs to be done... and does it.

Something to Think About:
What trend are you watching that just could be the next Big Thing in Five Years?

CHAPTER 6

INTREPID SPIRITS

> "Unlike the timid souls, intrepid spirits seek victory over those things that seem impossible
> *Ferdinand Magellan*

According to Merriam-Webster's Dictionary, an entrepreneur is, "a person who has possession of an enterprise, or venture, and assumes significant accountability for the inherent risks and the outcome." He or she may also be "an ambitious leader who combines land, labor, and capital to create a market for new goods and services."

While this sounds like a great individual, the Driscolls are not big proponents of the word "entrepreneur." Too often, people associate entrepreneurs with get rich quick schemes, reality TV shows, and huge risks like starting a business after business and selling business after business. It is surprising that people are proud to say they are serial entrepreneurs. Normally, serial in front of most words is not a good thing. A better way to describe an entrepreneur is someone who is successful at building a business and could take the accountability for all the risks that it takes to be successful. You might call this person an intrepid spirit.

> *The Sea is dangerous and its storms are terrible, but these obstacles have never been sufficient reason to remain ashore…*
> *Unlike the timid souls, intrepid spirits seek victory over those things that seem impossible*

It is with an iron will that they embark on the most daring of all endeavors, to meet the shadowy future without fear and conquer the unknown.
- Ferdinand Magellan

Entrepreneurs must be intrepid spirits. The world as we know it would not exist without intrepid spirits: those that take on the impossible and conquer the unknown. These intrepid spirits do not take on the impossible blindly; they attack with knowledge, thinking, strategy, discipline, and hard work. They commit. They are not of the get-rich-quick-and-move-on style.

There is a tendency to believe that the driving force for the modern-day entrepreneur is greed. But greed leads to failure. Dill has always been a believer in the cup being half full. There is plenty to go around. With his businesses, he never really worried about the competition. People were doubtful when they asked about *ignition's* competition, but the Driscolls responded, "We really don't know and really don't care." The Driscolls focused on what they could control - their business, their clients, their team. They always believed that if they did their best, always adding value for clients, then there was plenty for them and plenty for others. Many business decisions are made from fear instead of strength. Strength is always the best way to go.

There were decisions made in the Driscoll's businesses that others did not understand. They never let that distract them from their focus and their understanding. They stayed true to their compass, to their mission, to their goal. Some of those decisions had to do with giving up what they couldn't keep any way - great employees who had even better opportunities moving beyond their company. Celebrate them, and they will celebrate with you in the future. By always doing the right thing, you are gaining the one thing you cannot dare lose - your integrity.

> He is no fool who gives up what he cannot keep.
> To gain that which he cannot lose
> *Jim Elliot*

Starting a business is never easy. Susan was fortunate when they started *ignition*. She was naïve about the dangerous storms she might encounter. The good news was she had the knowledge, skill, focus, flexibility, and a desire to give it her all to be successful. By using the tools mentioned earlier, a plan - a real plan, not a pie-in-the-sky plan - testing the plan, figuring out a proper profit and loss for both the business and personally, the chances of success are improved. Starting a business is when the business owner must be an intrepid spirit and not give up too easily. Stay the course to truly give the business a chance to survive.

The success rate for new businesses is dismal. Therefore, create a confident atmosphere and act like a grownup business from the start. Use the tools. Ensure the new business is a place where the truth is heard. A business like that is a rare and special place. With that type of environment, politics go away, people feel like a functional, loving family, and the place is filled with forgiveness. Creating the right environment is a significant part of the business success formula. Of course, you must have a product or service that people think they want or need, but assuming the business has that, the rest is attitude.

If you create a culture where the leadership leads with questions, not answers, conducts autopsies without blame, and builds red alert mechanisms that cannot be ignored, the odds of success significantly improve in those early days. This leadership style will create a place where people feel safe and secure, where their ideas are valued, where creativity will flourish, and where the impossible will get done. That business will operate with PASSION (Poise, Attitude, Strategic, Substance and Style, Innovative, On Time and On Budget, Non-stop Forward Motion).

Following these principles will create a place where it will make a positive difference in people's lives and likely will make a profit as well. How can someone guarantee that success? Because the team will do its best to not fail. The team will recognize when their product or service is not relevant and will make the proper course corrections. The team will embrace change, not run from it. Team members will self-select, and the naysayers will vote themselves off the island as they realize they do not belong.

Something to Think About:
What does it mean to you to be an Intrepid Spirit?

CHAPTER 7

GO SMALL TO BE BIG

> The journey of a thousand miles
> begins with a single step
> *Lao Tzu (paraphrased)*

There are times when issues and challenges appear too big to overcome. Or we have a dream that seems too big, so we never start because it is too overwhelming. Dill often says, "How do you eat an elephant? One bite at a time." So how do you get started on your dream or overcoming a challenge? One step at a time. One hour at a time. One breath at a time.

The Driscolls have created global events by focusing on going small to be big. But what does that really mean? Here are a few guidelines to help you do the small things to make the big things happen:

Rule Number 1:
Know the difference between an idea and a product or service.

Ideas are a dime a dozen. They become a product or service only when real people are willing to pay full retail for them. When creating a business, know the difference. Ideas will not pay the bills. Even if you are one of the few lucky creative individuals who actually get paid to create ideas, if those ideas can't be executed or implemented, the business will dry up. The ideas must become reality.

Rule Number 2:
Revenue - Profit = Expense

The only number a business owner can really control is expense. This is difficult for many people to grasp, as they have not been trained in discipline. The entitlement attitude and the instant gratification society are killers of the discipline needed to manage expenses and sacrifice early in a business endeavor.

Rule Number 3:
The 6 Fs: Focus, Fear, Flexible, Facts, Finish, AND Fun!

It is amazing how many businesses lose their Focus and the next thing you know they are headed off the cliff with high debt, unhappy employees, and the feeling of disaster looming around the corner. It can get scary fast. Usually companies that lose focus do not understand their mission and core values.

Many people see *Fear* as a terrible thing, but it can have a positive impact in your life. A touch of fear in what you are doing creates an excitement everyday as you work toward your goal.

Flexibility is key. The world changes and at times the business must change as well. Look at Kodak, they created the camera industry, but they refused to become the new method of creating memories. With the proper flexibility, that company could still lead with their original mission of providing people with life long memories. But it lost focus along the way thinking their mission was the traditional paper photo.

It is important to always find out the truth about any situation. You must know the true *Facts*, not fake news. Doing this will create transparency in your life and business.

Believe it or not, *Finish* is one of the hardest. You don't want to be like former Cincinnati Bengals coach Sam Wyche. His team was happy to get to the Super Bowl, but couldn't pull off the win.

Make sure your team wants to win the Super Bowl. The last details, the last delivery, the last budget reconciliation, the last (you fill in the blank) is the most critical of all the activities. The finish, if not properly done, can totally erase all the goodwill done up to that point.

And the one in business most often forgotten is *Fun*. Life is too serious at times. There are no rules that state fun is not allowed in business and even in personal lives. Enjoy the successes, enjoy the small moments, have some fun. Studies have shown that happy employees are more productive.

THE SIX F'S OF SUCCESS:
Focus, Fear, Flexibility, Facts, Finish and Fun

Rule Number 4:
Stay balanced

Business people must keep balance in their lives or they will not be able to make great decisions. To keep a business heading in the right direction, great decisions must be made constantly. Without balance, most people will hit HALT:

H *ungry*
A *ngry*
L *onely*
T *ired*

HALT has been the demise of many businesses and programs. Back in July of 1990, Dill's company, McCann Erickson Event Marketing, was producing the Budweiser Steel Wheels tour. He got a call at midnight from Europe. The team was experiencing HALT. They had traveled around the world working diligently to keep Anheuser-Busch managers as well as the Rolling Stones happy. The hours were crazy; they had little sleep, and were feeling pure exhaustion. Dill did what great leaders should always do. He stepped up to help. He hopped on a plane, relieved the manager so he could take a couple of days off, and the next night Dill was hanging from the rafters in the Olympic Stadium in Barcelona, Spain installing Budweiser banners. The manager came back refreshed and ready to work harder for a leader like Dill that led from the front. Dill never asked his team to do something he had not done himself or would not at a moment's notice do himself.

Rule Number 5:
Never lie to your banker

He or she must be your best ally. More about this concept in Chapter 8.

Rule Number 6:
Always ask yourself if you are really doing what is best for your business, your family, and your community.

Something to Think About:
How will you stay humble and grounded when you have your first, second, and hundredth success?

CHAPTER 8

THE MAGNIFICENT SEVEN

> *It is impossible to begin to learn that which one thinks one already knows*
> *Epictetus*

Your banker. Your lawyer. Your accountant. Your insurance agent. Your financial advisor. Your mentor. Your spiritual leader. These are the Magnificent Seven that every business owner needs.

It is amazing to hear successful business people claim they are self-made. *No one is self-made.* People may be self-directed, self-disciplined, self-starters, and self-finishers, but no one is self-made. Ask any successful small businessperson and ask them who their key advisors were. Most likely you will hear at least four of the seven, if not all seven.

> *The easiest way for me to grow as a person is to surround myself with people smarter than I*
> *Dill Driscoll*

Banker

Through the years with every company the Driscolls have started, their banker was their best friend. Bank of Lake Placid, Lake Placid NY helped start Equipe Sport; Factory Point Bank, Manchester, VT helped start World Sports Promotions; Bank of Aspen, Aspen, CO continues to help World Sports Promotions grow; Clayton Bank, Clayton, MO was there for Momentum; Factory Point Bank, Manchester, VT started *ignition*; Colony Bank, Fitzgerald, GA gave *ignition* the growth capital it required.

The Driscolls prefer regional, local banks since they can personally know the President of the bank. Being close with your preferred bank means you can count on each other in tough situations. Once, Susan was in Vermont and Dill was in Germany. The company was growing and Coca-Cola had awarded *ignition* with a significant project. The challenge was *ignition* needed to spend over $1 million prior to Coca-Cola being able to pay any money. Susan was panicked while Dill, being the calm one in these situations, said, "No problem." From a street corner in Essen, Germany he called Dan Stannard, their banker in VT, explained to him the issue, and the next day their line of credit was increased to cover the cash short fall. It is in situations like this when it is important to know the banker.

The banker needs to know the good and the bad. There is a tendency to close communications with the bank when times are tough. But the best results occur when the banker has honest, consistent conversations with a business owner fully knowing the wins, the risks, and the challenges. Every year, the Driscolls shared their annual business plan with their bankers. This way the bankers knew what to expect. There were no surprises. More communication in tight cash times is much better than radar silence. The banker is more willing to work with a company when they know the truth and are provided with constant updates.

It is also important to pick the right banker. Unfortunately, some bankers enjoy their power, and it is more about wielding it over those that need to borrow money than wanting to share their customer's dreams and visions. Find a banker that you are comfortable with, not intimidated by, and is also excited about your business. Select a banker that understands your passion, but also will give you honest positive consultation.

> "A good general not only sees the way to victory.
> He also knows when victory is impossible
> *Polybius*

Lawyer

The Driscolls clearly remember the day they signed *ignition's* Operating Agreement in their lawyer's office in Atlanta, GA. Susan remembers feeling like they were getting married that day. The commitment and the dreams were huge, but they were feeling nothing but positive excitement and optimism. Ironically, 15 years later the same team was in the same conference room of the lawyer's office signing the papers to sell *ignition* to Havas Sports & Entertainment.

The role of a good business lawyer is to provide legal advice and assistance while representing his or her clients in legal matters. Some people think they can save a few dollars by incorporating their company with a simple online service or not at all. The Driscolls are strong believers in being professional and starting your company from day one with the right legal documents and representation. Eventually, you will need a lawyer.

Unfortunately in today's society, lawsuits are plentiful and if a business is active, odds are it will be sued along with its owners. Again, it is important to choose a lawyer carefully. Choose a person who is trustworthy, someone knowledgeable in the business industry, someone responsive, and someone affordable. Listen carefully to the legal advice, even though at times it is difficult to accept. As with the banker, make sure the legal representative who is chosen understands and buys-in to your passion and vision.

One of the worst memories for McWhorter Driscoll LLC was in 1998 in Atlanta, GA. The sheriff showed up at the door to deliver a summons naming McWhorter Driscoll LLC, Susan McWhorter, and Dill Driscoll as defendants in a $600 million lawsuit. The company was less than a year old, and it was already being sued. Not just sued, but sued for $600 million. At least they were in good company; the Best of the 20th Century was suing FOX Media and Rupert Murdoch as well.

Dill had met a man on an airplane a year earlier, and the man had an idea. It was a great idea for a television show for the turning of the century, which he called the Best of the 20th Century. Dill, with much excitement and salesmanship, took the idea with permission from the man to FOX. The programming and sales people at FOX liked the idea so much that the first two weeks of January 1998, Dill and Susan were presenting in New York to FOX's top twenty advertisers to sponsor the program. The idea got caught up in television politics, and the idea fizzled. Later, a similar program, or so the man who came up with the idea thought, showed up on TV Guide, which was owned at the time by Rupert Murdoch. Dill and Susan thought the man was their friend, but to sue FOX and Murdoch, he had to sue Dill and Susan as well. At least that's what his lawyer told him. The man had a contingency lawyer meaning the man paid nothing, and the lawyer got paid when he won the case. FOX and Murdoch have many lawyers on staff, so for them this was just another assignment. Dill and Susan, of course, did not have a contingency lawyer or a staff of lawyers. All they had was a lawyer from New York specializing in the industry at $300 to $500 an hour, which was quite expensive.

> The tragedy of war is that
> it uses man's best to do man's worst
> *Harry Emerson Fosdick*

The other thing about lawsuits is the defendant doesn't get to respond with his or her side of the story until way down the legal process and this process must be followed. The lawsuit process went on for a year, and Dill and Susan never got to tell their side of the story. But $150,000 later in legal fees, their lawyers finally wore out the contingency lawyer, since there was no case, and the man settled for $10,000. It went from $600 million to $10,000. The lesson learned from that experience early on was in most cases just settle. To this day, the Driscolls hate this principle, but a lot of emotions, pain, sweat, and dollars can be saved if you make an offer and move on. Unfortunately, this principle is training our society to sue. Be careful and pick the proper battles.

Accountant

Susan was a smart businesswoman and bid out to find the proper accounting firm. One of her best friends is an accountant, but she didn't want to give the business to her. She wanted to make sure she was being responsible and knew the market. It was a great process to go through, and her friend's firm was the best choice. With accountants, it isn't just the firm, it's the person. When Melinda, the Driscoll's accountant, moved firms, *ignition* moved with her. Melinda is a part of the family. She is an executor of their wills.

An accountant is someone who keeps, audits, and inspects financial records and prepares financial and tax reports. The accountant is there when the company or someone personally gets audited. In choosing an accountant, make sure it is someone that can protect you from the IRS and other government and regulatory entities. A company most likely will get audited whether by the IRS, its clients, its insurance company, or its bank. Other entities want to know that a business is being handled well, especially when it comes to financials.

Insurance Agent

The insurance agent is not a company's enemy. The natural tendency is to not tell the whole truth about the risks to your agent because it will increase the premium. However, when an accident, natural disaster, or a disgruntled employee strikes, if a company has planned properly, its best friend is the insurance agent and lawyer. Someone will get hurt, whether employee, vendor, or customer. Insurance is meant to protect a company against those risks.

Insurance is the act, business, or system of insuring. Simply, it's the coverage by a contract binding a party to indemnify another against specified loss in return for premiums paid. And premiums paid can be significant, especially if the company has several claims.

Most small businesses, believe it or not, tend to be unique in their risks. For instance, *ignition* in Vermont was the only business like it in the area. The insurance agent the company eventually used was an expert in the ski industry. When the company moved back to Atlanta, there were significant savings in insurance premiums due to the insurance agent there had the Olympics as a customer. With better understanding of the business, the insurance agent could better serve *ignition*. Find someone who understands your business and its unique risks.

At *ignition*, the team was thankful the company had the proper workers' compensation coverage when Brad, one of the team members, had a life-altering accident in Chicago at the racetrack. His family and the *ignition* family are forever grateful that even to this day, Brad is completely taken care of with the insurance covering his mom to be able to stay at home with him to tend to his needs. Therefore, an entity should have insurance to protect the company and the employees for a sustainable future.

Financial Planner

The financial planner is the most fun of the Magnificent Seven. This partner means the company is making money that needs to be invested. The goal of a financial planner is to help plan the work, work the plan. The financial planner is the head coach on guiding someone to a secure future, to prepare for the day when it is time to turn the keys over to the next generation and start another chapter in life.

Many things can go wrong with money. Trust is key in selecting the perfect financial planner. Understanding how the financial planner is compensated is critical to making sure his or her success is measured by the customer's success and not how many trades or other measures that do not help the customer, but helps the financial planner's boss.

Everyone has the next big investment, the next big thing to get rich quick. If it sounds too good to be true, most likely it is too good to be true.

Mentor

The terms mentor and mentee at times are over used and superficial; however, a true mentor is priceless. To get the most out of life, it is great to find someone who has a bit of wisdom to help advise. It is important to have a sounding board that is unbiased, has lived experiences that may help you prevent making a few mistakes. Truly great people have both a mentor and a mentee. The great person wants to help others and help the next generation. Amazingly, these relationships are most successful when they happen naturally.

Spiritual Leader

No matter a person's beliefs, having someone to share them with is an important asset to a balanced, content life. *ignition* was fortunate to have its spiritual leader, Max Helton, founder of Motor Racing Outreach, or NASCAR church as Dill calls it. He was there for everyone to share their joys, their fears, their hurts, and their celebrations. He helped people search for their own true meaning in life.

The Magnificent Seven - Seven people with seven distinctly different roles. One goal: To help businesses and the people behind those businesses win. Get the right team early in a business career and enjoy a life filled with a team that will become a part of the family for years to come. It is never too early to start finding your team.

Something to Think About:
Who are your Magnificent Seven?

CHAPTER 9

DON'T FALL IN LOVE WITH YOUR IDEA

> Nothing dies harder than a bad idea
> *Julia Cameron*

Do not fall in love with your business idea until you make a profit. Many people fall so deeply in love with their product they forget to be realistic about its potential for success. They also do not want to listen to others who have more wisdom that can help them be successful. Listening to other people who are smarter than you is hard. On the other hand, there are many examples of listening to the wrong people.

Fortunately, and unfortunately, the Driscolls have had many experiences working on both sides of this complex problem. Many times, the reason people get into a failed situation is they listened to the wrong people. Dill and Susan refer to it as "believing your own press." People get caught up in the positive news, mostly from family and friends who really don't know any better, that they do not listen to or encourage constructive criticism.

Think of taste. Something that tastes wonderful in one region of the country may not taste delicious in another area of the country. But it is so good, how can others not like it? Well, they just don't.

A great illustration is grits, which for years was a truly southern dish that northerners just did not understand. Today it is served in some of the fanciest restaurants in New York City. Grits are even hip.

Why did it take years for grits to become popular in New York City? Isn't it the leader for trends in the US? Most successes do not happen overnight, and it took a while for celebrities in New York City to fall in love with grits. Celebrities started requesting it, the famous chefs caught on, and then grits became popular.

The interesting thing about start-up businesses is most people think they are overnight successes. For Crocs, it took years before they were discovered; JC Penny took years before it succeeded. The common man doesn't see the entrepreneur scraping by, putting it all on the line for years, and hoping to make a decent living. But then there is a key point that turns it all around. It is unpredictable what that tipping point will be. It could be a celebrity finds it, retailers fall in love with it, a crisis happens and it is needed for the solution to the crisis. One just never knows when his or her day will happen.

There should be a course in every business school called, "The Art of Starting a Business," or as most hip schools call it, the "Entrepreneur Class." Caution: Starting a business will cause many sleepless nights and it may even cause poverty. It is not for the weak, and it isn't like the entrepreneurs that are portrayed on reality TV. It is arduous work that takes a significant commitment, risk, and a little bit of luck.

A great piece of advice is before jumping straight into your own venture, it is always a good thing to get some experience working for a successful company. It will give you the training to get it right on someone else's dime. But when someone makes it, which many do, it is important to remember where you came from. Remember the trials and give back. Always give back and you will be rewarded.

Something to Think About:
If you had to pick an industry to pursue a career, what would you choose and why?

CHAPTER 10

INTEGRITY IS ALL YOU'VE GOT

> He who walks with integrity walks with security
> *Proverbs 10:9*
> *(Paraphrased)*

Integrity is all you've got. It is the POISE we discussed back in chapter one. There are absolutely no degrees of integrity. You either have it or you don't. According to Merriam-Webster Dictionary, integrity is a steadfast adherence to a strict ethical code and the quality or condition of being whole or undivided. It can be made up of small actions or large actions. It permeates everything you do.

> You're looking for three things, generally, in a person: intelligence, energy, and integrity.
> And if they don't have the last one, don't even bother
> **with the first two**
> *Warren Buffett*

Coca-Cola had introduced a new Diet Coke flavor, Diet Coke with Lemon. Dill's creative idea to help introduce this product to the target market used the new Vespas, trendy motor scooters from Italy just being introduced to the United States. These were then painted yellow and a team of young people rode around and delivered ice cold Diet Coke with Lemon. The project went great, and the team finished the drill or so they thought. Several months later, the representative from Coca-Cola called and wanted *ignition* to deliver one of the Vespas to Los Angeles for a silent auction item.

Susan warned the client that the Vespas were used so they were not in mint condition. The client said it was no problem, just ship the Vespa. The charity raised the needed amount of money and a woman from LA was excited to have her Diet Coke with Lemon yellow Vespa delivered to her home. However, upon arrival, she was one very dissatisfied customer. There were scratches and nicks on this Vespa she had just paid over $6,000 for. The distraught client called and had forgotten he had been warned about the condition of the Vespa.

Susan quickly made the right decision based on the mission of the company and its integrity. "No problem," she told them, "We will send someone tomorrow to pick up the Vespa, repaint and decal the Vespa, delivering our LA customer a same as brand new Vespa." After spending $3,000 to make good on the promise, *ignition* had made the client happy. Two years later, the same client from Coca-Cola was working for John Deere and called *ignition* with a new project.

He told the account executive that the only reason he called *ignition* was because of the integrity Susan had shown when he had the Diet Coke with Lemon Vespa issues in LA. Integrity pays off.

> A good name is rather to be chosen than great riches, and loving favour rather than silver and gold
> *Proverbs 22:1 (KJV)*
> *Favorite verse of Truett Cathy, creator of Chick-fil-A*

On a larger scale, during the Vancouver Olympics, Dill and Susan got to meet and spend time with Karl Eller and his wife Stevie. Karl is the author of Integrity is All You've Got. He made a small fortune in the outdoor sign business, lost said fortune in the convenience store business, and subsequently recovered it in the outdoor sign business. The lessons learned from Mr. Eller those days in Vancouver were amazing and always helped Dill and Susan as they grew their own business. The secret is he had integrity. He shares several lessons in his book like the following:

Lesson 1: When he heard bad news, he did not have a knee-jerk reaction. He would go for a walk and think. As we know thinking is hard work, and it takes time, but it gives great rewards. He would also talk over situations with his wife. A listening ear always helps.

Lesson 2: He did not take the easy way out and declare bankruptcy. He did this because he knew that choice would significantly hurt others, especially his smaller vendors. He worked out a plan with each one that was willing to work with him and took on hundreds of millions of personal debts to keep his word to people.

Lesson 3: No matter how difficult situations may become, if you focus on what you know, in Mr. Eller's case outdoor signs, you can accomplish amazing things.

> A true leader has the confidence to stand alone,
> the courage to make tough decisions,
> and the compassion to listen to the needs of others.
> He does not set out to be a leader,
> but becomes one by the equality of his actions
> and the integrity of his intent
> *Douglas MacArthur*

Ernest Hemingway used one of his characters to say, *"Happiness in intelligent people is the rarest thing I know."* The Driscolls find that hard to believe. Intelligence does not preclude someone from having Integrity, and if you have Integrity you are on a path that brings happiness and a clear conscious. Just imagine a life full of lies. There will always be stress trying to remember to whom you said what. Maybe the better phrase is *"Happiness in people without integrity is the rarest thing I know".* How freeing it is to always tell the truth. There is no stress of having to remember what story you told to which person.

All great companies not only have integrity, but great service. The quality of service your company provides to its customers will be directly tied to the integrity you maintain in your business.

> **I never had a policy...
> I just tried my best each and every day**
> *Abraham Lincoln*

The following acronym will help you remember that integrity matters when in comes to service:

S *ervant leadership*
E *nthusiasm for opportunities*
R *espect for the customers*
V *igilant to always do the right thing*
I *nterest in, "How may we serve you?"*
C *ommitment to the company and customers' needs*
E *mployment - our jobs depend upon the customer's satisfaction*

> **Integrity cannot be taken from a person...
> it can only be given away**
> *Dill Driscoll*

> **And in the end, it's not the years in life that count.
> It's the life in your years**
> *Abraham Lincoln*

Something to Think About:
What is the hardest decision you have made in the last year?
Are you proud of that decision?

CHAPTER 11

YOUR PERSONAL PROFIT AND LOSS

*For what shall it profit a man,
if he shall gain the whole world, and lose his own soul?*
Mark 8:36 (KJV)

When people talk about *profit* and *loss* (P&L) or income statements most minds go straight to financials. However, a true personal P&L is more than the financial condition of the checkbook and hopefully savings account. It encompasses other core value areas of life.

At *ignition*, the team had three Ps - People, Planet, and Profit.

The true measure of bottom line success at *ignition* came from how the team treated people. Were they adding value or extracting value to their professional and personal life? How were they treating the planet? The team was encouraged to work from home at least one day a week. Think about the savings in fuel and pollution to the planet. Then finally, profit. Is the company making money and is it making it in a

---

PROFIT:

The return on a business undertaking after all operating expenses has been met.

LOSS:

The act or an instance of losing; The amount of something lost.

- *Merriam-Webster Dictionary*

a fair and ethical way? If so, then the people in the company can do positive things for humanity.

In a personal P&L, it is important to define the people. Are they family, friends, co-workers, teammates, community, or even enemies? With planet, ask what role can be played to take care of the Earth, a gift to us often taken for granted. Lastly, with profit, question what this means personally. Hopefully it is not just about the money.

As stated earlier, it is much easier to make a positive difference for others if money is being made. Those are resources that can be given back. The story goes that JC Penny failed many times in his life to start a successful retail business. But later in life, he finally figured out the formula for success, and at that time he began giving 10% away and keeping 90%. By the end of his career, it is told that he was giving away 90% of his financial gain and keeping 10%. That is making a positive difference in people's lives.

In today's world, it can be overwhelming to think about paying the bills, much less get ahead. However, there are simple steps and sacrifices that can be taken to get on the right path. Susan is a big believer in documenting everything that money is spent on. It is eye opening when someone tracks every penny they spend for a month and see where the money is going. They find out that they are spending $150 a month on fast food breakfast when purchasing a few boxes of cereal and milk for the month is much cheaper. They find out the $60 a month spent on cigarettes or Starbucks can go toward rent. Many times, the money is there, but the discipline to manage that money is missing. To this day, Susan still tracks where their money is being spent every month and how that expenditure is tracking against their annual budget. This is not only for their business, but also for their personal life. If someone cannot manage his or her personal P&L, why would a company entrust its P&L with that person? As in leadership, one must lead himself before others. In P&L, one must manage his own prior to managing someone else's.

Most people generally choose profit over loss, but not all people know how to accomplish profit. In business today, there are many complicated financial instruments and measurements. The Driscolls have found that keeping it simple works best for them. Early in their business and even as they grew, they took a simple formula to help build and manage their budgets.

Revenue - Profit = Expense
or
Allowance - Savings = Expense

Most people spend (expense) before they have any idea of their revenue potential and then cannot figure out why there is no profit. Part of business planning is having a realistic forecast of what real potential revenue can be, determining the desired level of profit, then managing your expenses to those numbers. It is amazing how this simple formula can help prevent overspending at the initial stages that cripples a business before it is even started. For those fortunate to have an allowance, there is no reason to not save. There is also no reason to overdraft. It is all about discipline and awareness of what you are doing.

A personal P&L is affected greatly by the willingness to dream. So many people just wander through life, which prevents the opportunity to dream. This is needed to establish goals, plans, and even disciplined time management. Put feet to the prayers and dreams. With a clear understanding of a personal P&L, the world is wide open. The Driscolls encourage people to dream big, to act as if the dream has come true, but don't spend the money that dream will bring you until the dream is reality.

> All men dream; but not equally.
> Those who dream by night in dusty recesses of their minds wake up in the day to find it was vanity, but the dreamers of the day are dangerous men, for they may act their dreams with open eyes, to make it possible.
> *T.E. Lawrence*

One of the greatest sources of revenue and expense for each one of us is our mouths. The right words in the right tone can add tremendous value to relationships (revenue). On the flip side, the wrong words in the wrong tone can damage relationships beyond repair (expense). Be careful how the mouth is used and when it is used. Most people do not realize the power of the mouth to build up or destroy.

**Something to Think About:
What five expenses can you cut by 20% over the next 90 days?**

CHAPTER 12

WHAT DOES YOUR SUCCESS LOOK LIKE?

> Not being afraid to confront one's fears is critical to one's success
> *Dill Driscoll*

Success can be defined in several ways. There are material measurements of success, but the more important measures are emotional and your contributions to humankind. Success can be summed up simply as achieving a goal, but in the world today, many people tend to judge success based on a person's wealth. This might be an abundance of money, fancy home and car, or more possessions than is needed.

Max Helton taught the Driscolls that there are four things that rob us of our peace, joy and contentment - Things, Circumstances, Others and the most important one, Ourselves.

Things
"I like her dress better than mine"
"I like his truck better than mine"
"If I only had more money, I'd be happy."

Circumstance
"My alarm clock didn't go off, and I let that ruin my day."
"There was a traffic jam, and I arrived late to my wedding."
"My children are sick."

Others
"Johnny just really irritates me, just his voice drives me crazy."
"My husband came home all grouchy, so now I'm grouchy."

Ourselves
This is the most important. If it's self-pride or self-pity, we are all self-centered. We choose how to respond.

> I cannot give you the formula for success,
> but I can give you the formula for failure - which is:
> Try to please everybody
> *Herbert Bayard Swope*

If people realize this, they can then make the choice to not allow these things to get in the way of their peace, joy, and contentment. The Driscolls think the greatest virtue that brings peace, joy, and contentment fastest is to forgive. Someone only hurts himself or herself if they hold a grudge. Let go and move on.

Success does not always happen the way we think it should. Dill was a kid who attended nine different schools in seven cities in four states, and he believed he was and is successful. But more importantly he believes if he can do it, then you can do it too.

During the Summer of 1975, Dill worked for Serge Lussi, owner of the Holiday Inn in Lake Placid, NY. Serge and his wife Caroline had bought the Holiday Inn in Wilmington, NY, when they were young. The hotel was already named the Holiday Inn, and the chain today called Holiday Inn had not started business yet. When the current Holiday Inn chain opened for business, they heard about the Holiday Inn in New York. They sued the Lussi's for not having permission to use their name, or so they thought. Armed with one of their members of the Magnificent Seven, their lawyer named Sam Whore from Boston, they stood strong claiming they owned the name first. The courts agreed and they won. To this day, they have a good relationship with Holiday Inn and still own a beautiful Crown Plaza in Lake Placid, NY.

While Dill was painting Serge's Holiday Inn, Serge gave Dill some advice. Serge told him, "Dill, you are 24 years old. You are a great coach and teacher, but this is the end for you in Lake Placid. You have a special energy, and you need to explore the world. Find the right thing for you." This was the push Dill needed to go see the world.

Dill believes people have until they are 30 to figure out what they want to do with the rest of their life. In 1981, Dill turned 30 and was Vice President of World Wide Ski Corporation. Susan at 30 was selected to lead the commercialization of one of the largest projects in The Coca-Cola Company history.

By 35, a person needs to be in place to make enough money to take care of all his or her family's needs. In 1985, Dill was 35, and World Sports Promotions was two years old and growing. Susan at 35 was on the cusp of founding *ignition*. By 50, a person needs to be able to do the next big thing.

Over those 15 years, Dill sold World Sports Promotions to McCann Erickson, founded Momentum and sold it to McCann Erickson, founded *ignition* and had several offers to sell it. Finally, in April 2012, they did sell *ignition* and started Susan's 3rd Chapter in life and Dill's 5th or 6th - they lost count.

Years:
18 - 30   *Explore*
30 - 35   *Vision Set*
35 - 50   *Building Stability*
50+   *Share Your Wisdom*

Dill and Susan, 61 and 49 respectively, were at a stage where they had the health and energy to start another chapter and give back to the future of their world with the students at the Stafford School of Business at Abraham Baldwin Agriculture College as the Co-Deans of the Business School. With this new adventure accomplished, they were continuing to remain relevant and could reinvent themselves.

> "If one is lucky, a solitary fantasy can totally transform one million realities"
>
> *Maya Angelou*

The path was not always full of roses. From 1977 to 1996, Dill had six children with three wives. To say the least, Dill didn't understand the family part at all. He was providing financially like a professional, but emotionally he had failed them miserably. In 1998, Susan McWhorter came into his life, and together as a couple, they have figured out how to be successful financially as well as emotionally and support their children and grandchildren while being a great role model and support system to a big wonderful family. The last 19 years have been a true blessing. The moral of the story is it is never too late to figure it all out. With the right attitude, focus, flexibility, and finishing the drill, peace, joy, and contentment can be obtained.

Don't ask, "Can I do it?" but "When do I start?" We can learn from other wise people that have walked on this world. Solomon in the Bible could have had anything in the world he wanted, but he asked God for wisdom. God gave him that wisdom and so much more! Searching for wisdom will always lead to a successful life filled with peace, joy, and contentment.

Something to Think About:
How might you change your behavior if you knew it would take you to where you truly wanted to go?

CHAPTER 13

THE STRATEGY TO GET THERE

> "You cannot build a reputation on
> what you are going to do
> *Henry Ford*

In 1983, Dill's vision was to build a global sports marketing firm, one that would make a difference in people's lives. There are several approaches to a vision like this - sit back and hope it will happen (most likely it won't happen), quietly work towards the vision while not sharing it with anyone, or, as only Dill does so well, go tell the world immediately what the company is going to be: World Sports Promotions. Proclaim World Sports Promotions not just US Sports Promotions? Out of Aspen, CO with not even one client? He did that. And guess what? World Sports Promotions within a couple of years was conducting business in Europe with Busch CitySki.

The company morphed into McCann Event Marketing, which became Momentum, a global marketing company. But one global marketing company wasn't enough, so Dill and Susan created *ignition*, a global marketing company. The world headquarters for *ignition* was located in Osierfield, GA (population 50).

> "We do not rise to the level of our expectations.
> We fall to the level of our training
> *Archilochus*

For a successful company and even a person's life, a clear *vision* and *mission* is critical. In 1983 the mission of World Sports Promotions was to make each person with whom they came into contact ask themselves, "Who are those guys!?" Why was that the mission of a business? The team knew it was out to create an entity that was truly special. In fact, the first day of work every employee would get an Apple computer. Remember this was in 1983 and Apple computers were not common in business. Everyone who was creative and cool wanted an Apple, but they were difficult to obtain.

The Apple computer was the company's recruiting tool, its *lagniappe*. This is a French/Creole term referring to "a little extra" of a product or service added at the end of a deal or sale. Commonly used in the street markets of Louisiana, it can be found in many places. A baker's dozen (the thirteenth donut) at the bakery or a fortune cookie at the Chinese restaurant can be seen as a sort of lagniappe. One of Dill's favorite is from Eye Peek, an optometrist's office in Lake Placid, NY. They give out tootsie roll pops to customers at the end of the eye exam. As you form a strategy for your future business, remember the lagniappe. It is an interesting *strategy* for distinguishing your business from others. Dill and Susan's lagniappe is to always add value and not extract it.

VISION:
The manner in which one sees or conceives of something
- *Merriam-Webster Dictionary*

MISSION:
An inner calling to pursue an activity or
perform a service - *Merriam-Webster Dictionary*

STRATEGY:
A plan of action resulting from strategy or intended to accomplish a specific goal - *Merriam-Webster Dictionary*

LAGNIAPPE:
A little something extra added at the end of a deal or sale.

The strategy for World Sports Promotions was to be the most creative agency in the world with the most motivated employees by creating a true family environment. The team understood The Art of War by Sun Tzu. This tremendous book of knowledge was written in China over 2500 years ago. The book begins with, "The art of war is of vital importance to the state. It is a matter of life and death, a road either to safety or to ruin. Hence under no circumstances can it be neglected." The book ends with "Hence it is only the enlightened ruler and wise general who will use the highest intelligence of the army for purposes of spying, and thereby achieve great results. Spies are a most important element in war, because upon them depends an army's ability to move."

> Victorious warriors win first and then go to war,
> while defeated warriors go to war first and then seek to win
>
> *Sun Tzu*

Business is a war. The best and the brightest business leaders understand the principles of war and operate their entities accordingly while always being vigilant to do the morally right thing. And, that, friends, is very difficult to do. There will always be temptations to cut corners, tell a little lie, stretch the truth, or try to get rich quick. However, the Driscolls guarantee you those temptations, if followed, will lead to the eventual death of a business or the soul of a person.

The legacy World Sports Promotions left from its humble beginnings was that it created many experiential marketing leaders. Young employees throughout the world who bought into the dream from the beginning could spread their wings to fly off to their dreams as well.

Something to Think About:
Write your mission, vision and your strategy to achieve them?

CHAPTER 14

POSITIONING YOURSELF

> *Positioning is not what you do to the product;
> it's what you do to the mind of the prospect*
> *Al Ries*

A positioning statement is not a statement about you, but rather a statement about what you do or the value you bring to your target audience. It is not a factual claim; it is a reason for people to want you on their team, to want to be around you. Your positioning statement will capture the essence of who you are, what you have done, and where you are going. And remember, if you do not position yourself, someone else will and it is usually not complimentary or quite accurate of the positioning you want to portray about yourself.

Dill's positioning is a creative problem solver with a global view who attacks every project with a sense of urgency and enthusiasm. As you begin to think about your positioning statement, remember, as time marches on this statement will change. Hopefully a person's core values only change in a positive direction.

It is much easier to look at brands both large and small to get a better understanding of how a person might think of his or her

---

POSITIONING STATEMENT:
A declaration that captures the essence of your company and what you provide for the customer.

own brand. There is a traditional format for brands to follow in their positioning statement: *For (target audience), (brand) of all (competitive framework), delivers (point of difference) because (reason to believe).*

> Where there is no vision, the people perish
> *Proverbs 29:18*

A brand does not have to follow this format exactly. However, it should capture the essence of the target, the framework, the point of difference, and why a consumer should believe that point of difference. For instance, look at Mountain Dew's statement: *For 16 to 24-year-old males, who embrace excitement, adventure and fun, Mountain Dew of all carbonated soft drinks, delivers great taste that exhilarates like no other because Mountain Dew is energizing, thirst quenching, and has a one of a kind citrus taste.*

This seems to be a mouthful, but it is effective. They launched the brand nationally using Channel One, a television network that played in middle schools and high schools across America. Bingo, right on target, and it remains the category leader to this day.

> Before you are a leader,
> success is all about growing yourself.
> When you become a leader,
> success is all about growing others
> *Jack Welch*

Let's take another path to creating a positioning statement. Ask these four questions. Give each question serious thought and begin developing the positioning statement that reflects the brand meaning. Let's use Dill's positioning statement for practice.

Question 1: Whose team do I want to be on?
To the top brands of the world

Question 2: Where do I play?
As a premiere creative problem solver

Question 3: Where do I win?
When there is a critical opportunity, which must be taken care of in short order

Question 4: Why should anyone believe you?
Because he creates successful marketing programs for the leading brands in the world, including Coca-Cola, Nestle, Delta Air Lines, Vodafone, Nokia, ESPN, General Motors, Live 8, Live Earth, Blue Planet Run, and more

Once positioning is established, then develop the elevator speech for when someone asks you the dreaded question," What do you do?" The elevator speech should be no more than 2 to 3 minutes long to explain in a clear, concise way what you do. It should be memorable and have one or two key take away points.

Something to Think About:
Write your positioning statement.
Write your elevator speech.

ELEVATOR SPEECH:
Short concise memorable speech to explain the nature of your business.

CHAPTER 15

FINISH THE DRILL

> What you get by reaching your goals is not as important as what you become by reaching your goals
>
> *Zig Ziglar*

What are the training tools available to us to really dig in and sort out where we are going? Get a great book that inspires you daily. The Driscolls first book is the Bible. It has many great lessons, and they read it every day (or at least try to). There are many great inspiring authors who get a person to think only positive thoughts that day. Inspiration and positive thinking are important to finish the drill.

At times you will get into the weeds. The question is how do you get out quickly? As we approach finishing the drill, let's take our life in segments. No one knows how long he or she has on this earth, but you should take a stab at a plan with the flexibility to pivot when needed. As the book started from day one - plan the work, work the plan (the positive way) or fail to plan, plan to fail (the negative way), having a plan will set a person free. To set goals and eventually meet them and occasionally beat them is freeing.

The Driscolls suggest the following course of action: Set a plan for your higher education or immediate post high-school transition to life - usually a two-year or four-year plan. What is my major, my minor, my certifications, my internships, my apprenticeships, my study time, my exercise time, my "me" time? You should plan now at the beginning and have a purpose. Don't just wander through college or technical training, or life because if you do, you will have accomplished nothing, but maybe a piece of paper stating you have a degree or a certification. So what?

Set a plan for your first five years of work. Dill's was crazy: Years 1 and 2, taught economics and humanities at Northwood School, coached soccer, skiing, and lacrosse; Years 3 and 4, started Equipe Sport, Equipe Foot, president of Lake Placid Business Association, ran a marathon, won the Stowe Sugarbush Lake Placid Challenge, had a son, and got divorced; Year 5, worked for Ski Hut Wilton, CT, Bloomingdales, NYC, and Carroll Reed North Conway, NH. What an exciting first five year. The plan was to experience as much as he could to figure out what he was going to do when he grew up. In those five years, he learned to teach, coach, and lead. He learned to pay the bills, bring ideas to life, and close the deals. Learning the importance of integrity, hard work, and being remarkable were skills that enabled him to create the business enterprises he did and lead them to success. By 1980, he was ready to seek the shadowy future without fear and conquer the unknown.

Annual Review of Plans and Pivot as Necessary. Remember "No Battle was won without a plan...our according to plan". It is important to annually review your goals, accomplishments, and short comings so you can redirect as necessary for the future. Continue to Build New Plans. Non-stop forward motion. As life goes through phases, new plans will be needed to keep you focused on living life as a success.

> Many of life's failures are people who did not realize how close they were to success when they gave up
>
> *Thomas Edison*

As we wrap up the lessons of life via business, it is the Driscoll's closing prayer that each of you wake up every morning and decide to be radiators, not drains; that you seek power through knowledge that leads to wisdom; that you remember to treat everyone the same

- with dignity and respect. If you can accomplish these principles, the Driscolls guarantee good things will happen in your life!

> Through knowledge comes wisdom, and wisdom leads to the true miracles of life
> *Dill Driscoll*

Something to Think About:
Write down your dream career…put it in a folder and review it every 60 days…are you doing the things to get you there?

WHAT WE HAVE LEARNED THROUGH THE YEARS

These are a few things Dill and Susan have learned over the years across the many adventures they have experienced:

The best classroom in the world is at the feet of an elderly person

When you are in love it shows

Just one person saying to me "you have made my day" makes my day

Having a child fall asleep in your arms is one of the most peaceful things in the world

Being kind is more important than being right

You should never say no to a gift from a child

We can always pray for someone when we do not have the strength to help him or her some other way

No matter how serious your life requires you to be, everyone needs a friend to act goofy with

Sometimes all a person needs is a hand to hold and a heart to understand

Life is like a roll of toilet paper.
The closer it gets to the end the faster it goes.

We should be glad God does not give us everything we ask for.

Money does not buy class.

It is hard to work in an environment where change is not embraced

Exercise is very important to one's mental health

Not being afraid to confront one's fears is critical to one's success

When you plan to get even with someone, you are only letting that person continue to hurt you

Real forgiveness breeds forgetfulness

Love, not time, heals all wounds

The easiest way for me to grow as a person is to surround myself with people smarter than I

Everyone you meet deserves to be greeted with a smile and treated the same

No one is perfect until you fall in love with them

When someone harbors bitterness, happiness will dock elsewhere

One should keep his words both soft and tender, because tomorrow he may have to eat them

A smile is an inexpensive way to improve your looks

Tomorrow everything will be bright and sunny IF you are focusing on positive thoughts. Speaking negatively about a circumstance, thing, or person will never lead to a good conclusion.
So why do it?

Those small daily happenings are what make life spectacular

Under everyone's hard shell is someone who wants to be appreciated and loved

To ignore the facts does not change the facts

Life is tough and the tough get going

Opportunities are never lost. Someone will always take the ones you miss

Teaching…not in it for the income…in it for the outcome Remember there are no mistakes…only lessons

Stick to what you know…and do it better than everybody else

Integrity cannot be taken from a person…it can only be given away

You have a choice everyday…be a radiator not a drain

Mathematically there is no such thing as giving more than 100%

A man is literally what he thinks

And we know that all things work together for good to those who love God, to those who are called according to His purpose Romans 8:28

Nothing ever becomes real until you experience it

The million dollar call almost always is made after the office is closed…answer the phone

DILL'ISMS

Poise - an attitude of confidence that comes from complete honesty. A belief in what you are doing is good for you and the customer. Complete trust in the mission.

Passion - Poise, Attitude, Strategic, Substance & Style, Innovative, On-Time On-Budget, Non-Stop Forward Motion

Plan the Work, Work the Plan

Go Small to be Big!

Stay low and keep moving!

Safety, Security, and Smiles! If it is to be, it is up to me!

The heart of the matter…is a matter of the heart!

Richly fill your role no matter how boring the task.
Act with intention. HELMET ON!

True heroes are humble and pass it on!

Inside out leaders live and promote truth, trust,
and teamwork, and they flourish everyone they influence!

Keep Diggin'

The adventure has just begun!

Go create you purpose and your story!

Bye For Now

ABOUT THE AUTHORS

> *Dill'ism:*
> "Poise is an attitude of confidence
> which comes from complete Honesty.
> A Belief in what you are doing will be good
> for you and the "client".
> Complete trust in the mission.

Susan and Dill are business consultants with a focus on marketing, team dynamics, and culture.

Mark "Dill" Driscoll is an internationally recognized visionary whose unconventional marketing perspective are fueled by his "passions of the heart." Dill's entrepreneurial spirit has spawned at least eight companies in a career bridging decades. He is the founder of industry breakthrough outfits such as World Sports Promotions, McCann Event Marketing, Momentum, and *ignition*. Today Dill is the driving creative solution force behind McWhorter Driscoll LLC, a global consulting enterprise. True to his all-encompassing marketing mantra, "bring brands to life in the streets, every day, everywhere," Dill and his teams have traveled the globe to deliver original solutions for activating some of the biggest brands on Earth.

Prior to being a marketing mogul, Dill was a Baker Scholar who taught high school economics, coached student-athletes, and owned and operated retail outlets. These experiences helped foster Dill's personal mission to create opportunities for young people around the world. So far, tens of thousands of aspiring teens and young adults have benefited from his talents and wisdom. His can-do attitude, innovative ideas, and exemplary leadership have secured this brand-building pioneer a place in marketing history.

Beginning in Lake Placid, New York, Dill's first venture was with Equipe Sport - a one-of-a-kind sporting goods store - where he created the world's first indoor track for customers to experience in real conditions the new Nike Waffle Trainers. Dill's intuitive sense of building brand relationships with consumers had begun its journey.

World Sports Promotions kick-started his profitable marketing path, taking Busch Beer and the Mountains to the people by building ski ramps throughout the US, including Summer events in Florida and later abroad. McCann Erickson later acquired World Sports, which became McCann Event Marketing. After five years of the "corporate" life, Dill became restless to put his visions into action again. Thus, Momentum was born, which is also now owned by McCann Erickson. To close his agency ownership journey, Dill and his wife, Susan, created *ignition*, a global marketing powerhouse that they operated for fifteen years prior to selling it to Havas Media.

Dill has worked in more than 60 countries on five continents with successful programs springing from his on-going leadership. Dill's combination of can-do attitude and groundbreaking innovative thinking, and his focus on passion and heritage, are the foundation upon which his companies continue to build lasting relationships for client brands.

Dill has served as the co-Dean, with his wife Susan, for the Stafford School of Business at Abraham Baldwin Agricultural College and was named the first Entrepreneur in Residence for the Terry College of Business at the University of Georgia. He has been a visiting speaker, and/or faculty member at St. Lawrence University, Georgia Technical Institute, Abraham Baldwin Agriculture College, and the Deer Run Fellowship Program. He has written two books including Cool Shoes:

The Experiential Marketing Playbook and Take Charge!, the textbook he uses to guide students and those ready to take charge of their careers and life.

Through his career, Dill has added value to companies and brands such as Anheuser-Busch, AT&T, The Coca-Cola Company, General Motors, Nestle, Marion Merrill Dow, Sports Illustrated, Delta Air Lines, ESPN, Vodafone, Nokia, AOL, Chick- fil-A, Bill and Melinda Gates Foundation, the USO, Blue Planet Run, Exxon, Blackberry, John Deere, Victoria Secret, Bacardi, BP, Embraer, eBay, United Nations Foundation, Kia, Honda, IndyCar, Live Earth, Live 8, Popular Science, and many more. Dill has worked on ten Olympics since 1996 and five FIFA World Cup Trophy Tours since 1998. Through his experiences with sports and entertainment he has served on the Entertainment Executive Committee for the USO creating a program that raised over $10 million for veterans since the inception.

Susan McWhorter Driscoll is a savvy marketer and enterprising business leader. She and Dill founded McWhorter Driscoll, LLC in 1997. Susan is co-founder of *ignition* and its creative arm, *ignition* Studios. As McWhorter Driscoll has grown, Susan has maintained responsibility for all financial planning and management of the companies that comprise their holding company. Since its inception and under her fiscal stewardship, McWhorter Driscoll has founded and / or added several properties to its holdings, including: companies like *ignition* Abroad, the parent company for *ignition's* international offices; MacGolf, a nationwide amateur golf tour; WeGotGear, a marketing premiums company; McWhorter Driscoll Farm; and key investments such as EvoShield, iScribe, and Surterra Therapeutics where Susan and Dill remain active investors and coaches. Susan is also on the corporate board of iScribe and Surterra Texas.

Her marketing career began immediately after receiving her Masters in Marketing Research from The University of Georgia when she joined The Coca-Cola Company in Atlanta. Susan spent ten years in the Coca-Cola system amassing numerous successes: she led the commercialization team of the 20oz. plastic Coca-Cola Contour bottle for Coca-Cola USA, was named one of Ad Age's top 100 marketers in 1994 and directed the marketing for the Coca-Cola sponsorship of the 1996 Olympic Torch Relay. This last project served as the stepping-stone to her involvement in unique grass roots marketing programs throughout the world.

Upon the sale of *ignition* to Havas Media, Susan became co-Dean, with Dill, of the Stafford School of business. Susan has guest lectured at the University of Georgia and Abraham Baldwin Agriculture College.

Recently, Susan served as President of Surterra Therapeutics with the key responsibility of leading the team to receive one of the initial five licenses in the state of Florida to cultivate, manufacture, and distribute medical cannabis. In two years, Susan led the team to win the license and then build a vertically integrated business from the ground up for cultivation, manufacturing, and retail facilities along with building an operational team to lead the industry with smart thinking, branding, and execution.

Susan has served as a board member of Worldspan, an international motorsports ministry; the Terry College of Business Alumni Board; Northwood School, Lake Placid, NY; the Ocilla/ Irwin County Chamber of Commerce; Ruth's Cottage for domestic violence; and the treasurer of her local church. She and Dill have also ventured into the world of motorsports marketing as a race team owner (placing 2nd in the Indy 500 four times in a row) and continue exploring new business opportunities and development for the collective companies of McWhorter Driscoll.

OUR STORY
WITH SOME STORIES
FROM THE ROAD

Mark "Dill" Driscoll was born to be different and to make a difference in people's lives. He just didn't know it.

It was early one morning in Steamboat Springs, Colorado. The University of Colorado Ski Team was up early to prepare for the Steamboat Winter Carnival Giant Slalom race to be held that afternoon. With those early morning preparations for the team, Mark had some time to get into some mischief. It was the Winter of 1959, and at eight years old, he had already been travelling with the "big boys" for two Winters. Dave Butts and Bob Gray, members of the University of Colorado Ski Team who lived with the Driscoll family just off campus in Boulder, would watch out for the young lad on these ski trips away from home. As any other eight-year-old would do, Mark wandered downtown Steamboat by himself. This was his lucky day, there was going to be a skijoring race. This is where a horse with a rope pulls a person on skis; it is about a 400-yard sprint. The fastest time wins. So being a quick thinker ready to compete, he convinced the gentleman running the event to allow him to enter. After all, he was scheduled to forerun the big slalom race later in the day so this should have been a piece of cake. Mark learned early in life that you are always closing a deal, and that is what he did with the race organizer since children were normally not allowed to race. As the time to race neared the "big boys" from the University of Colorado Ski team arrived and saw Mark getting ready to be pulled. Worried somewhat about their little mascot, they yelled to the rider pulling Mark to remember that he was just a little boy. As the horse took off, it yanked small Mark and he flew into the air. The landing wasn't pretty. He landed flat on his face, and with determination he did not let go. The morning paper featured the little boy who would not let go - bloody face and all. "Tougher Than Nails" was born on that day. Early miracles happened in Dill's life that day as well. The doctor at the ER thought it was a miracle that the ice and snow had not torn his face off. Over those early years, there were many crazy events that shaped Dill's life ranging from horrific car wrecks, ski wrecks and even fires that would shape him to be the generous, survivor he is today. Dill continued to travel the world alone for years until he met his sunshine, Susan.

Now we advance forward a few years when his family began breaking apart while they were living in the wide-open space of Montana. Mark decided to deal with the family pressure by selling his first Coca-Colas for the Billings Mustangs Minor League team with the St. Louis Cardinals, skiing competitively across the West, and working on the Kamphe Ranch in Luther, Montana. When the rest of the family moved back to Connecticut, Mark stayed behind. For three months, he worked miles away from civilization with the only contact to the world being a two-way radio. He learned about nature and demanding work during those days. Finally, his mother sent for him to return to New York. At twelve years of age, he boarded the train alone for the three-day journey back East.

But the survivor didn't give up with that twist in his life. He continued to dream of skiing and continued to train by "skiing" on a 300-foot hill in Connecticut; climbing back up and skiing back down hours at a time. He actually cut saplings to make slalom gates for his ski hill. Finally, the break came - if you can call it that. On Mark's thirteenth birthday, his dad left the family for good. His dad had gone from riches to rags and ended up living for a time below Grand Central Station with the other homeless of New York. That fateful birthday was when Mark decided he had to be a survivor, find a way out and give his mom one less mouth to feed. Finally, when he was fifteen, through the support of the Maxwell family, who began a search for the prodigy skier that had disappeared at such an early age, Mark (soon to be known as "Dill") was introduced to Lake Placid, New York, home of the 1932 and 1980 Olympics.

It was an early Summer morning and Little Mark, yes being he was 15 and only 5'2" and not ready to have that growth spurt yet, leaves New Rochelle, New York on a Trailways Bus with all his belongings - a small duffle bag of clothes. He spends all Summer living with Warren Witherell, a famous ski coach from Northwood School in Lake Placid, New York, helping him remodel his home and working at Northwood readying the school for Fall classes. Getting excited for the school year to start, it is a beautiful Adirondack morning when the Headmaster wakes Mark up and tells him to pack his bag. "You are going home. No room at the school." Paying students were the priority, and he wasn't one of those - even though he had worked all Summer for free. Northwood School is a great school for academics and Winter athletes. Several US ski team racers and NHL hockey players spent their high school years at Northwood.

What devastation, rejection at its best. But Mark didn't give up. He just kept diggin'. A new Headmaster arrived and through divine intervention heard the story of Little Mark Driscoll. John Friedlander, retired Green Bay Packer linebacker, realized the injustice that had been done and was determined to make things right. It was on another warm New England Summer day, when Mark got the call. "If you are willing to work all Summer again, be first in your class, be a leader, and work chores and wash dishes during the year, you will have a bed and place at Northwood" exclaimed Mr. Friedlander with that imposing stature of his. Mark couldn't pack fast enough and catch that Trailways bus one more time. He spent the Summer working with Bill Kelly, the head maintenance man, preparing the school once again for another promising school year and building Northwood a great baseball field.

The Trailways bus pulled up at Ormby's newsstand. Freddy Friedlander as the youth affectionately called him personally was waiting for young, little Mark to arrive. The first words Mark heard were the challenge that set him apart for his four years at Northwood. "You must be first in your class or NO Sports, and you will repeat the 9th grade." Dill was one of the first outliers. Well if you haven't figured it out yet, sports were Dill's life. The solution - be first in his class. Dill was an exceptional student; he made the grades and excelled at sport. The reward was team captain and class president positions that he earned over the years from his fellow students.

At an early age, Dill understood the Golden Rule. Do unto others as you would have them do unto you. Upon completion of high school, Dill was declared a Baker Scholar. The Baker Scholarship was established to train young men to be entrepreneurs. Dill took those lessons to heart and truly has represented what the Scholarship stood for through his years. The reward for being a Baker Scholar was full tuition for an undergraduate degree and then a MBA at Harvard. The "Powers that Be" decided that Dill should attend St. Lawrence University.

Short side story: *During Mark's high school years, he read constantly about John Dillinger, a 1930s American outlaw. Dillinger intrigued Mark, not because of his crime, but because of his capability to do the impossible. The FBI would appear to have him surrounded, but somehow, he escaped not once, but several times through his career. With Mark's focused intrigue, his teammates penned him "Dill" due to his capability to do the impossible in the classroom, on the field of play, and just out having fun. And the name stuck throughout life, because of his will to do the impossible in all his endeavors.*

Dill's skiing career continued through college, and he had the opportunity to coach in France and Switzerland in the Summers. That was the beginning of his positive influence on over five continents today. Life again wasn't always smooth for Dill. Being on the cusp of the US Ski team, Dill needed $5000 to go to Europe and train. It was known in the Ski team circles, if you don't train in Europe, you won't make the U.S. team. Coming from a family background that had significant wealth - you think "wait a minute, I thought he was poor" ... his mother and father had lost everything, but his family roots owned a significant publishing company at the time and were millionaires in the 60s... he had never asked them for anything, he decided to ask. They said NO. To this day, this has been a life lesson for Dill; wealth is fleeting. Life is more about people and compassion for them, than wealth and the material things it buys.

With the disappointment of not having the opportunity to compete for a spot on the US Ski team, Dill at the request of the Headmaster of a near bankrupt Northwood began his career as a teacher of Economics and Humanities as well as soccer, skiing, and lacrosse coach. Now keep in mind, there was a scholarship to Harvard for a MBA, but Dill chose the path of returning what others had given to him. That first year of teaching, Dill made $100 per week; but the contributions to the kids were tremendous.

It was the middle of Winter, a group of young guys were sitting around a fire figuring out what else can they do to make more money, but still live their passion - skiing. The team dreamed up the idea of a ski retail shop that was unique and different from any other ski shop in the area. Thus, Equipe Sports was born. With three other partners, Red LaFountaine, Bob McDermott and Michael "Twig" McGlynn, they built the premiere ski and sports retail business in Lake Placid. The team constantly dreamed of ideas to make their store different and appealing to the customers. They served beverages and snacks around the store fireplace after their customers came in from an exhausting day of skiing. They opened the world of preparing skis so the customers could see what was being done; in the past the ski preparation had been completed behind closed doors. This store is considered one of the places where Experiential Marketing began in its modern-day form.

One day a gentleman showed up at Equipe Sports selling his wares out of his trunk. "I've got the greatest new running shoe like none other." It was this shoe that looked like it had been made with a waffle maker. It had little nubs on the bottom. To feel the technical innovations of the shoe, a person needed to take a trial run wearing the shoes. There was a problem. The customers were wearing down the nobs, so the next customer thought it was a used shoe. There had to be a solution - an indoor running track in the store. Thus, the Nike Waffle Trainer was featured in their store with the first ever inside running track in a retail store in North America. This business grew into a nice, profitable entity upon which Dill sold his shares and decided to see the World. Well his partners told him, they would pay him $5,000 in cash, but he had to leave town that night. They didn't want any competition from him by staying around and opening another store. So, he packed up his pickup truck, and headed to the City.

Another short side story: *Experiential Marketing really started with God. He prepared the tablets and called Moses to go tell the people the rules. So, Moses went down the Mountain and said "Yo, I saw God and I have the rules on how we are to live." (Dill street language version) A movement was born through experiential marketing that has lasted for centuries.*

Dill's next stop was The Maxwell Family's Ski Hut in Wilton, CT then Bloomingdales in NYC, and Carol Reed in North Conway, New Hampshire, and finally working with Bob Beattie building NASTAR, the largest sports recreational sports program in the world at one time, where he learned more about retail and general business. But the real fun started next.

It was 23 December 1983 when Dill had a meeting with Bob Beattie who was the owner of Worldwide Ski Corporation. On that snowy Winter day in Aspen, CO after a disappointing reaction from his boss of bringing him a $500,000 endorsement deal in 1983 (that was huge), Dill practiced what he preached. If you don't believe in the mission of your job, you should move on to something else. Therefore, he quit, and decided to control his own destiny along with God's guidance. World Sports Promotions was born with a dream of being global and making a positive difference around the world. He began his business with no capital, just a business plan and a prayer.

The next day he called Ken Phelps the President of San Marco Ski Boots and asked him for an assignment. Ken needed someone to help him organize a national sales force. At the time Dill did not realize it but it was the first project of thousands over the next 32 years that would take him around the world many times over working on some of the most famous brands in the world. The Winter of 1984 was devoted to setting up San Marco by Spring; mission accomplished and it was on to the next project.

Two gentlemen from San Diego had developed a computer program that allowed you to serve on a tennis court and based on speed and location it gave you a score, based on your age you would win a gold, silver or bronze medal. They called it the National Serving Competition or NASCOM and they needed someone to make it into a reality. Dill was their man, because he had spent three years running NASTAR, The National Standard Race for skiing. He moved to San Diego and set a plan in motion that Spring and Summer that had NASCOM on center court of the US Open with all the stars of the day competing. It was that day that Dill met Mark McCormack who founded sports marketing as we know it today. Mark asked Dill to join International Management Group on several occasions over the years. After the US Open Dill turned NASCOM over to the team as he had another life changing phone call.

The call was from CB Vaughan of CB Sports, a very successful skiwear manufacturer in Bennington, Vermont. The ski business was on challenging times and in need of an idea to grab the attention of the non-enthusiast. CB asked Dill to join him and create a special idea, that would allow people to experience skiing on real snow not the rolling carpets that were the fad of the day. What they came up with was to test building a ski area on the Boston Common that December. They would name it CitySki. Now they just needed a sponsor. Dill used his Rolodex to reach out to Joe Corcoran, Brand Manager of Busch Beer. The idea fit the strategy of Busch Beer and Dill was literally off to the races. In mid-1985 Bill Post suggested that CB was too busy running CB Sports and that Dill should take 100%

ownership of World Sports Promotions. It was a terrific break for Dill as he would move the company back to Aspen. From late 1985 to 1988 World Sports Promotions operated out of Aspen. Anheuser-Busch kept the company busy with Busch CitySki, Michelob Light CityBeach, Natural Light CityFish and local projects. It was in late 1987 that Jack MacDonough with Anheuser-Busch suggested that Dill relocate World Sports Promotions to either Dallas or St. Louis as Aspen was "bit too much in the fast lane for people to take him seriously." So, it was decided that St. Louis was to be the new home. No sooner did they arrive in St. Louis than the opportunity to sell World Sports Promotions to TBWA occurred.

It was heady times for Dill as TBWA was an international advertising agency, and they were the first to realize that what Dill was creating would become a large part of the revenue stream of every major advertising company in the world. While Dill was mulling over their offer, John Dozier, a friend and employee of Dill, reached out to Art Tauder who worked for McCann Erickson. Art too saw the opportunity and convinced Dill and John to come to New York and meet with the top McCann executives. Boom! Dill walks in the conference room and there sat John Dooner, who had dated Dill's cousin Rosemary Ridder. It was like old home week. McCann wanted to do a deal but they dragged it out over the entire Summer. Dill had to ask Anheuser-Busch if it would still do business with him if he sold. They said they would but no new business until the deal was complete. As the deal dragged out Dill's bank account was going dry. It was the longest 4 months of his life.

On 15 September 1988 Dill signed a deal which was another game changer. McCann bought 100% of World Sports Promotions for $100, but it gave Dill a five-year employment contract, great salary, with stock and several bonus pools. Dill was to go and build McCann an experiential marketing firm to be proud of. From 1988 to 1993 Dill poured his heart and soul into the company. In 1989 they renamed it McCann Erickson Event Marketing and Dill and the team went out and built a client base second to none. Anheuser Busch, Coca-Cola,

AT&T, Marion Merrill Dow, General Motors, Sports Illustrated, Nintendo, Six Flags over America to name a few. During those years Dill also travelled the globe doing creative work for McCann clients in Europe and Central and South America.

In fall of 1993 the five-year employment contract was expiring and Dill looked around him and felt the McCann had become more about the money than about the idea and the execution of world class experiential marketing programs. So Dill did what he felt was the only thing to do but leave and moved to his attic at 19 Warson Terrace and started the Driscoll Company. In less than 48 hours the phone rang and it was another game changer. His old friend Sergio hollering at him to get to Atlanta as he needed an idea, Coca-Cola needed the big idea to push Pepsi out of Blockbuster. When Dill arrived at Sergio's office he asked "what are you calling the new company?" Dill said The Driscoll Company and Sergio said he was not hiring a company by that name and he better have something great by the morning along with some initial thinking on Blockbuster.

As Dill was running to the airport to catch a flight back to St. Louis, he called his good friend Bill Stolberg and asked him to meet him in the attic at 10 pm. That night after a couple of cold beers Dill and Bill named the new company Momentum, and the initial idea for Blockbuster was the Blockbuster Coca-Cola Movie Critic who would be syndicated in every major newspaper in America. Sergio liked both Momentum and the movie critic, and Coca-Cola became the new soft drink in Blockbuster, and at the end of the day they never used the movie critic.

Over the next 18 months Dill built a team that went out and changed the way several companies implemented their experiential marketing programs. In 18 short months Dill hired a core team of Erik Petersen, Andy Cook, Bill Meyer, RJ Nelson and Emmitt Cook. The client base was terrific, Coca-Cola, Anheuser Busch, and Nestle to name a few. A couple of projects really set Dill on the way.

The O'Doul's sampling program was so successful that the brand went from dead last to first in its category in 12 months. Dill was brought into Anheuser-Busch and asked why no one liked the product. He took a case back to the office and began taste testing at different temperatures. Dill went back the next day and told the brand manager if they sampled the product at 38 to 42 degrees Fahrenheit it tasted fantastic. Dill immediately wrapped a 24-foot refrigerated truck with taps on the sides and took off to Golf Tournaments. That first truck was so successful that by the next Summer they had 4! Again, a simple idea that made a difference.

Sometimes Dill found his ideas initially ended up in another direction. During these years, Dill helped Pacific Marketing Group in San Francisco sell to DMBB. Through that experience, Wes Shell introduced him to Michael Cookson. Michael and a group of people had the idea for a travelling interactive sport pavilion called SportsLab. Dill worked with the team in raising capital, design, construction and implementation. Two key players were on that team who would prove to be key in a phone call Dill would receive after SportsLab failed. Dan Moali and Haven Riviere became good friends with Dill through the entire SportLab journey, as well as Billy Packer. In late Summer of 1994 Dill received a phone call from Chuck Fruit, Vice President of Worldwide Sports and Entertainment at the Coca-Cola Company. "Dill we have a problem, Doug Ivester is upset with our proposed budget for Coca-Cola Olympic City, we are at $50 million and he wants to spend less than $15 million! Please bring your team to Atlanta ASAP and help us solve this." Dill sprang into action, four phone calls, Dan, Haven, Billy, and Michael. 48 hours later they were in Chuck's conference room getting briefed. They had ten days to get back to Chuck with a plan for Coca-Cola Olympic City. They did and the project was complete on time and on budget. It was an enormous success and today the World of Coca-Cola sits on the site in Atlanta.

In June of 1995 Dill got a phone call from John Donner asking to set up a meeting with Tony Pace. John was now Chairman of McCann and wanted Dill back in the family. Momentum was exploding and they knew that Dill needed back room help. As the good Lord would have it that September day when Dill met Tony in Atlanta at the downtown Ritz to talk in earnest about McCann acquiring Momentum, Dill got the call from Stu Cross telling him that Momentum would be leading the 1996 Olympic Torch Relay. The next day Dill met with Susan McWhorter and Robin Smith to confirm the deal.

When Dill arrived to meet with the Momentum team and plot out the next year which included the Torch Relay and Olympic City, they came to the reality that they needed back room help. It was with trepidation that Dill agreed to sell Momentum to McCann in the Fall of 1995. They agreed to change the name of McCann Erickson Event Marketing to Momentum and for Dill to move to New York and work with Tony Pace to grow the business. As Dill was planning the Olympic Torch Relay, he realized that McCann was probably not the right place for him. 1996 and 1997 flew by with Momentum buying Mark Dowley's Advent and Tony Pace moving on. Everyone wanted to pit Dowley against Dill but that just was not the case. Dill spent a week a month in South Africa from December 1996 to December 1997. Business was great but the bloom was off the rose. Dill had moved his family to Greenwich, Connecticut when one evening he had a call with Jim Heekin the President of McCann North America. Dill asked Jim why a $100,000 payment was late and he informed Dill that he was a "pain in the ass." Two days later Dill informed John Dooner that he would be leaving Momentum on 31 December 1997. It was mid-October and Dill had 75 days to figure out a way forward. At the time his marriage was in a tough straight and he had six children that he was not about to miss any payments. He had to get a plan together quickly and be prepared to execute it flawlessly.

The first person he told he was leaving was Scott McCune with Worldwide Sports and Entertainment at The Coca-Cola Company. Scott said, "Hang in there, I just might have a special project for you." The second person he called was Susan McWhorter who was now running the worldwide Coca-Cola account for Momentum.

Within 45 days of those two calls things became very clear. Scott wanted to do a test event with the FIFA World Cup Trophy, and he felt Dill was the only person he could trust to take the Trophy to Riyadh, Saudi Arabia. Dill picked the Trophy up at the FIFA House in Zurich during December 1997 and flew from Zurich to Paris to Riyadh. It was an amazing trip that proved to The Coca-Cola Company the power of that Trophy. The second event that happened was Susan and Dill formed McWhorter Driscoll LLC in November of 1997.

On 5 January 1998 McWhorter Driscoll officially had its first meeting at Coca-Cola; as always Sergio wanted a new name. On the spot Dill said they would be *ignition* as you needed *ignition* before Momentum. They dispatched Dill to Lagos, Nigeria to begin planning the 1998 World Cup Trophy Tour with a Replica Trophy. In 1998, Mike "Twig" McGlynn took the Replica Trophy to 12 countries. Dill had quite an experience in Lagos; disarming a Militia pickup with six soldiers firing rifles in the air. In 2002 FIFA would not give Coca-Cola the real Trophy so the team passed, in 2006 Coca-Cola and *ignition* took the real FIFA World Cup Trophy to 36 countries; in 2010, 81 countries and in 2014, 90 countries. Dill will never forget the first trip to Riyadh, alone with the replica Trophy in a Coca-Cola bag. Today it flies on its own 737 in a custom Louis Vuitton case!

Over the next 15 years, Dill and Susan had quite a ride with some of the most amazing brands in the World with *ignition*. There are too many special experiences to name them all, but there were also many Intrepid Spirits who made it all possible.

Susan's life was quite opposite of Dill's. She grew up in a stable, faith based home in rural South Georgia. The family never moved, and her parents still live in the home where she grew up. Her daddy is a Farmer, and her mama is a Homemaker. She learned lessons from living on the Farm about the cycle of life with animals and plants. She learned about great work ethic, long hours, and doing what it takes to help the crops grow and the animals live. She learned about compassion, generosity, and helping your neighbors. She had lots of "family" from the family's church and friends.

She always did what was expected - made great grades, went to college, and got a job. It just so happened the job was a dream job; Marketing for The Coca-Cola Company. She got her real break when she was thirty to lead the commercialization of the 20oz. Contour Coca-Cola Bottle. Prior to that, all plastic bottles for all soft drinks were generic. She led a male dominant team, all more experienced than her and paid more than her, to figure out the technology, the logistics, the financials, the marketing and the sales potential to introduce this new package to the US market. Her team leadership became a model for most effective teams at The Coca-Cola Company. She understood lead from the front, surround yourself with people that know about areas you do not know, lead with integrity, and lead with fun, focus, and finish.

But then she met Dill; thanks to Coca-Cola and the 1996 Olympic Torch Relay. In one year, she obtained a mortgage on a house, quit her corporate job, and began a business with this crazy guy, Dill. But she has never looked back. She has built her stories the last fifteen years with Dill as they have traveled the world together making a positive difference in people's lives through commerce.

Dill and Susan have started and owned several companies - *ignition*, a global marketing company; *ignition* Studios, a creative design company; *ignition* Europe, an experiential marketing company focused on European businesses; The Event Department, an experiential marketing company based in Essen Germany; Relay of Heroes, a marketing company focused on matching charities to business partners; WeGotGear, a specialty merchandise company; KTM, a business office park; STATS, a baseball practice tool company; Click-It, the first digital event photo share platform, and a few others primarily focused on helping the young, majority owners start these businesses. The common link is that these companies were started with no capital and with a mission that whatever the company does, it is to make a positive difference in people's lives.

Over the last 10 years, Susan and Dill have been making a positive difference with young people at ABAC (Abraham Baldwin Agriculture College) at one point as the Co-Deans of the Stafford School of Business and with students at the University of Georgia where Dill was named the first Entrepreneur in Residence for the Terry College of Business sharing their values, passions, and experiences to help guide these future leaders of our country.

As you will see, Dill has succeeded with the mentality of a warrior and survivor with no dependence on anyone, but his relationship with God. Susan brings her calmness and quietness to the team so that they complement each other when taking on the challenges of life. We hope this book, gave you courage and basic principles for you too to be the successful person in life that you were created to be.

Enjoy some Stories from the Road where you may find them to be just entertaining and you may also learn some marketing tips and business tips along the way. Godspeed.

1996 OLYMPIC TORCH RELAY

It was the Summer of 1984 and Dill was living in Coronado, California. It was few days before the Los Angeles Olympic Games were to open, and the Olympic Flame was to pass right in front of his condo. There was much anticipation as the Olympic Flame was soon to arrive for the Opening Ceremonies in LA. As the Flame approached, there was no warning, and it was gone before the spectators realized what had happened. Dill told his friends that evening that if he ever had a chance he would show a company how to share the Olympics with a country. Little did he know that he might just get that opportunity of a lifetime.

September 1994 St. Louis, MO

"Dill, come quickly! Sergio is one the phone!" Dill prayed for these calls often as he knew when the mercurial Chief Marketing Officer from Coca-Cola called he wanted big ideas, and Dill had delivered often for the Boss.

"Dill I need you here immediately to discuss how we activate the 1996 Olympic Torch Relay. We need a big idea quickly as we must decide if we want to purchase the rights." Dill smiled broadly and told Sergio he could be in Atlanta at 10h00 the next morning.

"Come with an idea"

"Yes sir."

It was a long night wrestling with what might work. Dill remembered that Bud Light ambushed the 1984 Olympic Torch Relay with the famous television ad of the farmer in a wheat field standing and clapping as the Olympic Flame passed. To this day people in marketing talk of that ad.

10h00 Sergio Zyman opened the door and in his typical fashion said "Dill, what do you have!" The idea was simple...Sergio lets share the Olympics with America for 84 days...from LA to Atlanta. We will create a rolling street party. We will have trailers in front of the Olympic Torch playing music, selling ice cold Cokes, and donating all proceeds to charity.

"Great! We need to buy the rights. Our team will get back to you when we have secured the rights. Safe travels home...and thanks again Dill"

A few months go by and Dill gets the Christmas present he will never forget. He was sent a Request for Proposal (RFP) to bid against other agencies for his idea. He was crushed. How can this be? Dill decided to sit on the sidelines. Not a day went by that he did not pray for the miracle that Sergio would overrule any committee and let him and his team at Momentum execute his idea.

And as Al Michaels says, "do you believe in miracles...Yes" Dill got the call one afternoon while he was in a meeting at the Ritz Carlton in downtown Atlanta. Stu Cross, VP Coca-Cola, phoned and said that he just left a meeting with Sergio and that he was told to tell Dill that the Torch was his to bring to life. Report to Coca-Cola in the morning to get started and meet Susan McWhorter, Marketing Director for the Olympic Torch Relay.

Dill and the Momentum team spent the next seven months planning minute-by-minute, street-by-street details on exactly how Coca-Cola would spend the 84 days leading up to the 1996 Olympics Opening Ceremony sharing the Olympics with America. The eighty-four days were amazing. Every team member shared the vision and mission, and it was said by many that Coca-Cola lit up America. It was an amazing ride.

Dill, Susan and their team have been executing the Olympic Torch Relay for Coca-Cola ever since. Rio marked the tenth Olympiad.

DRIVE AMERICAN QUALITY

In August of 1992, Bill Noack, Director of Corporate Communications for General Motors, summons Dill to his office in Washington, DC. Upon arrival he is instructed to sign a document swearing that what he was about to hear will not be discussed with anyone outside of a small circle of people. On that day, the planning for Drive American Quality began. It was a game changing top-secret project that involved four separate groups that historically did not play well together. The team competed daily for hearts, minds and pocket books of the American consumer. On a steamy hot evening there were representatives from General Motors, Ford, Chrysler, and the UAW crammed in a hot conference room. Bill introduced Dill and he laid out Drive American Quality.

The US Council for Automotive Research had done a massive survey to find out what every American already knew. The quality of the American automobile was horrible. The only way for Detroit to survive was to drastically improve the quality of the product and prove it to the world.

What Dill said was that the only solution was to take forty autos from each manufacturer...put them on Capitol Hill...invite the President of the United States and all of Congress to a test drive. Come and show the world that American Quality was back. The team selected 25 - 26 May 1993 as the date they would Drive American Quality. The team had ten months to plan this extraordinary event. Ten months to work with people who do not get along...who all have to be the smartest person in the room. It was a challenge but not really...Dill looked at it as an experiment. Dill hired David Alexander to work with him as the director and they just made friends with the entire team. After all, they were all saving Detroit!

On 26 May 1993, Robert Eaton CEO Chrysler, Red Poling CEO Ford, John Smith CEO General Motors, and Owen Bieber CEO The UAW were on Capitol Hill awaiting The President of the United

States. Up the street walks President Bill Clinton...parked in the middle of the street were a Corvette, a Chrysler, and a Mustang. John Smith (GM) was paying Dill's fee and felt that he was obliged to get POTUS to drive the Corvette. The entire press corps was assembled to take the historic photo that would be on the front page of newspapers around the world. At exactly 11h00 EST Bill Clinton got in the MUSTANG! Red Poling (Ford) was elated and John Smith gave Dill the stare! Heck everyone knew Bill "Bubba" Clinton was a Mustang guy! (being that 26 is Dill's lucky number and it was 26 May he thought he might have gotten lucky...no such luck)

Most of Congress also took a test drive that fateful day as well as the over 200 consumers and press. It was a success. History shows that from the Spring of 1993 the quality of the American automobile was back.

Boom! Plan The Work, Work The Plan.

This event really taught the team how to take a tough crowd of marketing professionals and give them a project that was bigger than anyone in the room and make it a success. After all, saving Detroit was a rallying cry people could truly believe in.

GOGO, MY WALKIN' PUP

Hasbro had a problem. GoGo, My Walkin' Pup was supposed to be the toy hit for Christmas. Yet early sales were not trending well. It is September and Wayne Charness, EVP of communications at Hasbro at the time, placed a call to Dill. "Red alert" we need you to create another hit. He told Dill of the lagging sales of their projected hit, and asked for an idea that needed to be executed immediately across the United States.

Like Hollywood the toy business is in the hit business. For movies it is the Summer blockbuster. For the toy business it is the Christmas hit. So GoGo was a key piece of revenue pie for fiscal 1992. The team had to create a hit to reach the numbers.

Dill had a crazy two-pronged attack…Dill said, "we walk the dog!"

Client was amused…where he asked…Dill's response was in every major shopping mall in America…hire 12 to 13 year old girls to walk the dog on the weekends in the top thirty markets in America…and it was doing its job…people were amused to see a cute battery operated dog walking and softly barking…the buzz was created…now for the second prong…move them off the shelves…Dill hired 20 year old models to walk the dog…where the dad's worked and played and dads would know what their daughters were talking about…the girls and dogs turned heads…BOOM…the team sold every GoGo My Walkin' Pup! RJ Nelson, RIP, was amazing helping lead this team!

Twenty years later Dill finally got his GoGo…his wife found them on sale again at where else but Walmart!

The lesson here is great planners have a sense of urgency…time is of the essence!

BUSCH CITYSKI

It is the Fall of 1984 and Dill gets a call from CB Vaughan who founded with his wife CB Sports, a successful skiwear company. The ski industry was experiencing a decline in ticket sales, and CB has an idea. Let's bring the mountains to downtown Boston, and Dill is crazy enough to take on the job. CB, Bill Post and Dill formed World Sports Promotions in September of 1984. Its sole purpose was to produce a world-class ski event on 20 December on the Boston Common, America's oldest Park.

They had an idea with no money, no permits, and no staff. Dill said a prayer and called Joe Corcoran the brand Manager of Busch Beer. Head for the mountains head for Busch Beer was their tag line, and rumor had it they wanted to expand the brand to the northeast. It was a match made in heaven; the team worked with every A-BI account, and if the account put Busch Beer on tap, they got to enter a team in the Busch CitySki Bartenders Cup. Bars loved it! The team now had a paying sponsor...they had the startup money needed to attract other sponsors.

Next Dill reached out to the city of Boston to get the necessary permits and was told there was no way a beer would get sponsorship on the Boston Common. Enter Tom Kershaw, owner of the Hampshire House, which happens to be the bar the TV show Cheers was based on, and Dottie Curran, the special events czar for the city. Dill agreed to raise money for the Special Olympics and to help put Christmas lights up in the Park. Permission granted; the permit was obtained!

Next Dill rounded up a team of ski folks to build a ski area that would be open for one day. Scott Reichhelm led the team and Nasohba Valley, a local ski area, brought out the snow making equipment. The team was ready to make snow on 10 December. But Mother Nature had other plans...it was 70 degrees! The press was out every evening reporting how the team was running out of time to build Busch CitySki. The entire city knew the plight. Publicity for Busch was tremendous.

December 19 Dill is at the kickoff party at the Marriott Long Wharf. The decision to cancel the event was moments away when BOOM! Dill saw a fishing boat motor past. "Dottie where is the ice factory?" Dan Mullen right down the street. Dill told Dottie to tell the press Busch CitySki would begin at 09h00 in morning, and ran out the door to order 125 tons of crushed ice.

Dill and the crew worked the entire night hauling and spreading 125 tons of ice. When the sun rose on the morning of 20 December, there was a ski area complete with ramps. The media showed up and BOOM! The story became global. The brand Dill was launched in the marketing world…much like Ghostbusters…got a problem or task that seems impossible, call Dill.

Lesson…leaders never…ever give up…

As Dill says…stay low…keep moving!

SPORTS ILLUSTRATED SPORTS FEST

One Fall Dill was invited to meet Bob Pitman the founder of MTV and at that time the President of Six Flags. Time Warner had just purchased the theme parks and they wanted to get some synergy with some of their other properties. Dill, as was becoming the norm in his career, was there to come up with an idea that was both BIG and small budget. It had to be portable, as the event would travel to six markets and it had to fit in multiple footprints.

Dill came up with the Sports Illustrated Sports Fest. It was 100,000 square feet of interactive sports for teenagers. The team built relationships with ESPN, NFL, MLB, NHL, NBA, MLS and the local teams in each market to provide celebrities. No one thought this would be possible! Each market had its own set of Challenges.

Atlanta was the opening market. The team had 10 days to build the entire venue. It was brutally hot and on day five it rained and rained...the entire venue was swept away. Dill's team was devastated. There was no way they could rebuild 100,000 square feet in five days. UNLESS...there was a new plan. That evening Dill coined a new phrase -- "Plan the work, Work the plan." The team was divided into small SWAT teams each tackling a specific area. Every 45 minutes the entire team regrouped to hydrate and check each SWAT team's progress...it was remarkable how the venue grew out of the asphalt while at the same time the team's feet were literally blistering from the extreme temperature off the asphalt. The event was opened on time to a rousing crowd. Park management including Bob Pitman felt that they had witnessed a small miracle. Dill told the people there that morning to never under estimate the power of truly committed men and women.

The rest of the tour was equally brutal. Houston the team was sprayed with bug spray from above...Dallas and Chicago intense winds were blowing down the displays, Los Angeles the heat was oppressive and finally New Jersey was, well, just New Jersey.

Dill's team leader on the project was John Dolan, later founder of his own very successful experiential marketing agency.

The lesson here from Dill was Focus…Flexible…Finish…Fun!

DELTA JULY 2003

Dill gets a call from Chuck Fruit, Vice President of Marketing at The Coca-Cola Company, telling him he was at a high-level marketing meeting at Delta Air Lines and he recommended him to Deirdre Hannett. Deirdre was brought into Delta to boost the morale as Delta was not a happy place to be. Pink slips were being issued and the speculation that bankruptcy was just around the corner.

Delta needed a dose of Dill's positive human energy. So, a brief arrived to the team. It was quite simple actually...Dill reminded the marketing committee of the importance of Delta Air Lines to Atlanta. We needed to remind the Atlanta consumer, who was hopping on AirTran, of the history of Delta and Atlanta. You see Delta Air Lines had a choice. It was between Birmingham and Atlanta. By choosing Atlanta as its headquarters, Delta allowed Atlanta to blossom and Hartsfield to become the busiest airport in the world. So how would Dill give his history lessons?

He told upper management that nothing was more important on Friday nights in Atlanta from August to November than High School football. Dill said that employees would send in the three reasons why their high school should be presented a $500 check at halftime for their school. The employees would pass out small footballs and remind Atlanta that indeed Delta Air Lines was part of the fabric of Atlanta. They thought Dill was nuts...this will never work! Well over 20,000 employees participated...morale picked up...business picked up...Dill was right...you communicate the truth...times are tough... but we will survive...we do not control the cost of fuel...we do control the lines of communication.

15 September 2005, Delta Air Lines filed for bankruptcy...30 April 2007, they came out..

ignition lost $500,000 on 15 September 2003 for payments lost in the Delta bankruptcy. After bankruptcy, *ignition* was the only agency in the marketing department still with Delta Air Lines who was there prior to their bankruptcy. The lesson here: Great leaders communicate with honesty and total transparency.

EQUIPE SPORT LTD

In the Spring of 1976 Dill, Moses LaFountaine, Bob McDermott, and Mike McGlynn opened a specialty ski, tennis, and running shop named Equipe Sport Ltd. It was indeed a special place that rewrote many rules of how a retail operation could and should be run. The founders had a tremendous belief in their products and services. Equipe only sold Nordica ski boots and Look Nevada ski bindings, which at the time Salomon had a 75% market share. But Salomon was a double pivot design and was not as safe as the single pivot Look. Today all bindings are single pivot. Equipe put in the first CB Sports boutique which at the time was thought to be crazy, as CB was notorious for a lack of product or late delivery. Dill and Twig fixed that problem, they would drive the 3 hours from Lake Placid to Bennington, Vermont in a pickup truck and back it up to the factory doors to get the orders. Another break through was back in 1976, you never let the customer see you working on their ski equipment; Dill and team said that they needed to let their customers see Joe Kempa and their equipment magicians work. They acquired the first "wet Belt Sander" in North America and put glass around the workroom for the entire world to see. BOOM! People came from Montreal and all over the Northeast to have the Equipe team help them with their ski gear.

The Summer of 1976 also saw Dill meet a salesman with a product that would change his life. The man arrived with a pickup truck full of boxes. Each box contained 18 pairs of shoes. He gave the pitch to Dill and team that they needed to be the first in their area to be selling these shoes which appeared to have come out of a waffle iron. The name of the company was Blue Ribbon Sports. Dill and team bought the box and immediately began having their customers try them on. Problem was the customer had to be on a hard surface to feel the waffle effect. Customers would go outside and scuff the new shoes. They sold them all, and the shoes all fell apart but the Equipe team felt BRS was on to something. That Winter Equipe bought a building on Main Street in Lake Placid and put a store called Equipe's Foot, and to be certain there were no more scuffed shoes, they put a state of the art Tartan indoor track so people could try on their shoes. In 1978 Blue Ribbon Sports changed its name to Nike. The shoe...the Nike Waffle Trainer. Dill saw the power of experiential marketing at Equipe and never looked back...

Winter of 1977 Bob Arrix from Capital Sports walks into Equipe on Saranac Avenue. He was looking for Dill as Lake Placid was to host the 1980 Winter Olympics and marketers were flooding town looking for an idea. Campbell's Soup was Bob's client and he was sniffing for ideas. Dill had one. As a ski racer and coach for over 20 years he had spent many a freezing day on the side of a mountain, and as a kid had fought forest fires using a tin back pack called an "Indian tank". It was a simple metal backpack with a pump to shoot water... Dill said let's shoot hot tomato soup out of the tank! Bring the soup to the cold skiers and workers and you will have a hit. Boom! People loved it...to this day people are still using "Indian Tanks" to deliver hot and cold beverages with the human touch!

Thank you, Moses, for leading the way with the human touch.

GAME BALL RELAY

It was the Spring of 2012 and Dill had his Team 14h30 students from the University of Georgia down for their annual trip to the farm in Osierfield. On Saturday evening after dinner they were all sitting on the patio discussing Georgia Football. Dill and Susan are season ticket holders, and at the time, went to every home game. Dill made the comment that Sanford Stadium was not full, the statewide passion for Georgia Football was waning especially in South Georgia. It was decided that night that Team 14h30 was going to work with McWhorter Driscoll to reignite the passion for the DAWGS! How you ask? Dill told the team we were going to use another tried and true idea…he told the team we are going to take the Game Ball for the opening game and run it 24/7 around the state arriving at Sanford Stadium precisely 10 minutes before kickoff and present the ball at midfield in front of over 90,000 screaming DAWG fans. Think Olympic Torch Relay…meets…FIFA World Cup Tour…meets SEC Football.

Dill had been doing these types of relays since 1994. It was a no brainer. The team set up a meeting with Allen Thomas, Associate Athletic Director for External Affairs. Dill, Susan, Wes Van Dyk, a recent graduate who also played football, and John Jones, a MBA student, pitched their statewide Game Ball Relay idea. Allen was worried that IMG, the company responsible for marketing UGA Athletics, would be nervous letting Team 14h30 take on such a big event. Hence it was cut back to a 24-hour relay from the Shepard Center in Atlanta to Sanford Stadium. The team launched at precisely 12h00 with the 1980 Championship Team carrying the ball the first 5 miles. The GBR passed through Centennial Park, CNN, the State Capital, Stone Mountain, Loganville, Snellville, and Monroe and into Athens. Highlights included Chance Veazey, a UGA baseball player who spent time at the Shepard Center, throwing out the first pitch at the Atlanta Braves game to kick-off the Relay and then Chance, Charlie Trippi and Vince Dooley carry the Game Ball to the 50-yard line to a thunderous ovation. There was not a dry eye in the house.

The idea also had a fundraising component. Wes, John and Dill thought the best way to raise money the first year would be to create a special club known as Red Zone Warriors. They printed up 500 shirts to be sold at $100 per shirt raising $50,000 for the Shepard Center. The team sold 403 shirts for a total of $40,300, in just two weeks! Dill believed that the Game Ball Relay truly had legs and could capture Georgia's imagination. Allen and IMG felt differently and banned Dill and the team from repeating the GBR in 2013. The St. Louis Cardinals and Cardinal Glennon Hospital borrowed the idea and branding without permission and did a GBR in the Spring of 2014. Dill to this day feels that the Game Ball Relay is a terrific vehicle to galvanize a community around their team. He believes the idea is not dead for UGA it is just taking a nap! But remember change is scary and even to big organizations.

COCA-COLA CHRISTMAS CARAVAN

It is September of 1996 and the Olympics for Dill were over. He had put the group together for Chuck Fruit to build Coca-Cola Olympic City, he had developed and executed the Olympic Torch Relay, and he worked with Mark Dowley, an executive with Momentum, on the AT&T Olympic program. It was the hardest year he ever lived. Dill's life would never be the same. Sergio Zyman called and asked Dill what he would like to do that fourth quarter for Coca-Cola. He thought back to the night in Detroit when the Torch went through the rough neighborhoods and how the kids just loved the Coca-Cola trucks and Harley-Davidson motorcycles. These neighborhoods were under marketed to by the brand. Again, he thought of an icon delivering ice cold Cokes with a special gift for these kids would create memory points to last a lifetime.

Boom!

Dill asked Sergio if he could build a 48-foot tractor-trailer with the Sunbloom Santa, light it up like a Christmas tree and from Thanksgiving to Christmas travel America hitting the neighborhoods where the families could not afford to go to the Mall and get a picture with Santa. Sergio liked the idea and off Dill went. He created the trailer with craftsmen out of St. Louis, Missouri and hired a Santa and an Elf to drive the truck and set up a small Christmas scene for Santa. They spared nothing that first year; the Santa suit was $5,000! The Truck appeared in parades, at schools, high school football games, and Walmart parking lots. That first year over 20,000 Polaroids were taken with children on Santa's lap; it was magical. Choirs came out and sang Christmas carols, dance groups performed and Coca-Cola and Dill again were beaming ear to ear. The public relations were terrific, but most importantly the team created memory points that to this day, Dill has people send him notes of thanks.

This Christmas will be the 21st year of a program that grew from one truck to five in America and is run in many countries around the world. The lesson here that resonates and always will is take the right icon and match it with the proper strategy and the consumer will come and the brand will make a memory that a human will never forget...the Human Touch! Ask yourself if you remember seeing the Coca-Cola Christmas Caravan...the Olympic Flame...the FIFA World Cup Trophy...a Coca-Cola Harley and ask yourself did you have a smile on your face...as Coca-Cola says...OPEN HAPPINESS!

The key learning here is to keep it fresh and keep it simple! Be willing to take a chance on that crazy idea that just may change the way you think. Or as Dill likes to say, Go small to be big!

THE EVENT DEPARTMENT

It was a damp and dreary Monday afternoon in October of 1999. Dill was in the parking lot of Coca-Cola Germany in Essen. David Haines the Chief Marketing Officer hollered across the lot to come see him in the morning. Dill and Susan had been hired by Coca-Cola Germany to work with the marketing group at Coca-Cola on building an experiential marketing team to regain market share. Coke had hired an experiential marketing agency in Germany that had done sampling for Coca-Cola in the past, but there was no world-class agency at the time in Germany. Dill was to train them. There was a lot of money on the table for this agency to take the coaching. Dill had travelled the world teaching agencies the proper techniques of serving ice cold Coca-Cola at 3 degrees C. But the Germans would have none of it. They believed that no one would like ice cold Coca-Cola.

The Saturday before, Dill had hired the agency to sample 50,000 Cokes in 5 markets. In Germany there are very few ice houses. It was a relatively new concept. As is his usual, Dill found the best icehouse and had everything set for Saturday, except the Agency instructed their employees to not use the ice. The Company had spent tens of thousands of dollars on ice that just melted in parking lots. Hence the meeting Tuesday morning with David Haines. He wanted Dill and Susan to open a marketing company in Germany to handle 75% of the Coca-Cola sampling / experiential marketing.

Susan was not in favor for all the right reasons. They did not have a working knowledge of how business was conducted in Germany, they did not have a magnificent seven fluent in German, (Banker, Accountant, Lawyer, Insurance Agent, Financial Planner, Mentor, Spiritual Leader) and lastly, they would have to spend a minimum of one week a month in Germany. BUT... as always, Dill saw this as an amazing opportunity and he had struck up a friendship with Mike Silberbach who owned one of the biggest ice companies in Germany, and we would need a lot of ice. That Tuesday evening, at Omero's, the Driscolls' favorite restaurant in Essen, the relationship was formed with Mike to take on this opportunity. He was excited. He said he needed 24 hours to get a team assembled. 24 hours later the new team was standing in the lobby of Omero's, and Mike introduced Joachim Bernstein. Joachim would run the books, Mike would run operations, Dill would run the account, and Susan would keep the team on point. The Event Department was born! They gave each of them 33.3 per cent of the new company. The key learning here is they should have had it be Susan 25%, Mike 24%, Bernie 24% and Dill 27% so the he and Susan would have had controlling interest. Be careful before you give too much away. Really consider the unintended consequences down the road. In business planning, plan for the worst and work hard to make sure only the best happens.

Dill and Susan would spend a week a month in Germany for four years. They hired Brian Murphy to be their on- the-ground-man to teach everyone how to operate with the Driscolls' best practices. It was a difficult job to say the least but Murph did an excellent job.

They had a terrific run with The Event Department creating all sorts of special activations on behalf of Coca-Cola Germany and its many brands. In the fourth quarter of 2004, Susan and Dill gave their third of the company to the team in Germany. The travel had finally worn him out and when he was not there, he could not assure the work and the money would keep coming.

The key lesson here is you must be a great coach, (Thanks Murph) you must have the right people, and the team must listen. When this is happening, you can create magic. And they did.

CLICK-IT

It was the Summer of 2001 and Dill got a call from the brand manager of Diet Coke with Lemon, a new product at Coca-Cola USA. They needed a unique experiential sampling program. The target audience was women 25 to 40. The challenge was where do you find this target when they would be most agreeable to sample ice-cold Diet Coke with Lemon. The short answer: in Super Market parking lots on hot days.

Now Dill needed the "Pixie Dust". At that time, the Internet was really taking off. Dill knew just the right guy to call -- Andy Burdick. Andy was a very creative person who Dill had collaborated with many times over many years. Dill felt that if he could match the Internet to a "human touch" activation, they would have a winner. In steps Nick Cianciolo, a technology wizard. The idea was to take a picture of someone, give them a code and they could go to the Internet in 6 hours and download their picture and share it with friends. My how times have changed since then.

The next day, Dill sold this idea to the brand Manager and Click-it, the company, was born. Dill and Susan gave them the startup capital for a 10% stake.

Now for this to really work Dill needed to create a photo op that the target women would love. It just so happened that while in Germany Dill noticed the resurgence of the original Vespa. The Piaggio Vespa, and women were riding them all over Europe again. So, the perfect photo op would be on the Vespa...a yellow Vespa to match the Diet Coke with Lemon logos.

The Summer and Fall of 2001 five teams armed with a 24'-straight truck, custom yellow Vespa, lap top with camera connected, and ice-cold product hit the super markets of America. The target audience loved the product and the idea of getting a picture on a special Vespa that they could share with their friends on the Internet. The kicker was when they shared photos it was framed in a Diet Coke with Lemon virtual frame.

15 years later Click-it is still being used by *ignition* and many other top marketing agencies...the good news is the technology has progressed where now they are posting immediately with small cameras and cellular technology and sharing globally with social media.

Key learning here is that Dill was always experimenting with things that would take others a year or two to accept, and he always surrounded himself with people who were experts in their field and let them do their job. And if it meant a new business being established, then let's go for it. That is an entrepreneur.

TAB CLEAR

It is October and Dill's phone rings. It is his old friend Sergio Zyman again. "Dill, we must kill Crystal Pepsi. It was clear! We had trained the world that all cola drinks were brown!"

Sergio did his magic; he had the Coca-Cola Chemists design a clear diet cola drink patterned after Tab. That Summer, Tab Clear was created to be a category killer.

Sergio's plan was to act like The Coca-Cola Company was absolutely serious about growing Tab Clear into a major brand. He had a stunt in mind which he told Dill was "right up your alley". The largest travel day in America is black Wednesday. Every major airport in America is jammed packed with our consumers, and they are on the move and thirsty. What a great surprise and delight to try an ice-cold Tab Clear.

Dill's challenge was getting permits to sample 1,000,000 Tab Clear's in the six busiest airports in America was going to be impossible on the highest traffic day of the year. As fate would have it Dill had a business relationship with Mark Abels whom worked at Fleishman Hillard with Dill on the Busch CitySki and then moved on to TWA before landing at Northwest Airlines. Dill called Mark and convinced him that if he let him sample Tab Clear on Northwest Airlines concourses the press would be overwhelmingly favorable for him and Tab Clear. He agreed and Dill had less than 30 days to operationalize a six-market sampling blitz with each airport averaging 166,666 ice cold drinks over a 12-hour period.

BOOM! 25 November 1992 Dill and team sampled 1,000,000 weary travelers across America. In December Doug Ivester announces a national rollout, 18 January 1993 he announces the UK rollout, March he announces the rollout in Japan, the competition united and in early 1994 it is discontinued. Mission accomplished category killed with a minimum investment. The team went Small to be Big. Sergio and Doug completely fooled the entire marketing community with a little stunt pulled off by the man who was notorious for pulling off the impossible...Dill

Key learnings here are always treat everyone the same. Dill had not worked with Mark Abels in years but he remembered Dill and his way he treated his team. Lastly be known as the "guy" who never gives up the good fight and delivers the impossible, with POISE and integrity...Dill made a career out of it! And small actions can appear big when properly communicated.

NATIONAL ASSOCIATION OF RECORD BREAKERS

1990 Wayne Charness, the Vice President of corporate communications for Hasbro, needs an experienced outside of the box thinking marketer who can execute the plan that the team comes up with. Wayne had worked at Anheuser-Busch prior to Hasbro and knew that they did all sorts of outside the box programs. Wayne was told to call Dill Driscoll and he did. The next thing Dill knew he was on a plane to Tokyo to see a Japanese phenomenon. They arrived on Friday and caught their breath as Saturday was going to be a busy day. They were going to go to several of the busiest shopping malls in Japan. What they saw was thousands of young Japanese kids racing battery operated slot cars on elaborate tracks. Wayne and Dill were blown away. There was a big idea here and Dill wanted to be a part of it.

The toy business, like Hollywood, is in the "hit" business. Every Christmas season you need at least one. Wayne and Dill felt they had a hit on their hands. The team at Hasbro named the car Record Breakers. On the flight home it dawned on Dill that Japan had no sanctioning body for the races. BOOM! What about National Association of Record Breakers…NARB…NASCAR for…kids…Dill really felt that this could be an on-going property, but Hasbro reminded him the job was to create a hit. And that they did.

Dill and the team created from scratch five super tracks that allowed them to be in five different markets each weekend. The teams would work seven days a week as they would put on major races on Saturdays with hundreds of kids competing from the top prize of a $1000 US Savings Bond. Each race was complete with a pit crew dressed in official NARB gear along with special mechanics to help the kids get more speed out of their Record Breaker. The real fun was the team produced a NARB television show each week from a select market. It was magic. Jesse the Body Ventura was the color and Keith Apple was the play-by-play man. The shows aired on cable and that made NARB appear to be BIG.

Hasbro had their hit and Dill had another notch in the belt of creating a national program in just weeks and executing it on time and on budget. God continued to smile on a company that truly believed anything is possible when you give glory to God.

Key learnings here were for a program this large Dill needed his Magnificent Seven.

- Banker for the proper financing
- Lawyer for trademark
- Accountant to help manage the large budget
- Insurance things will happen with this many moving parts... The same truck went under a low bridge twice!
- Mentor to keep Dill focused
- Spiritual leader to keep Dill humble
- Financial Planner because Dill realized early he would need one if he could keep wheels on the company

BLUE PLANET RUN

2005 was a year to remember for Dill, Susan and *ignition*. They executed Live Eight -- a global concert to create pressure on the G8 to relieve one billion dollars of debt. On 2 July 2005, Harvey Goldsmith, Bob Geldof, Kevin Wall, Dill and Susan watched live at Hyde Park, London while millions around the world watched streaming video on AOL from 7 venues around the world. It was truly magnificent. Later that Summer a gentleman walked into Dill's office on Means Street in Atlanta right behind The Coca-Cola Company Campus. It was a day that would change many people's lives.

Jin Zidell informed Dill that Jeff Seabright and Cindy Ann Hersom over at Coca-Cola told him that there was only one man who could organize a run around the world on the 40th parallel going 24/7 and he was lucky as Dill was right across the street. Jin had a vision of creating a stunt that the entire world could embrace and tell the plight of all the people around the world that did not have safe drinking water.

The stunt was a 94-day 24/7 run around the 40th parallel with the message of $25 USD provides safe drinking water for a person for life. The first thing Dill and his team did was convince Coca-Cola to fund the feasibility study. They graciously agreed and Dill was off to the races. Before seeking sponsors, Dill laid out a tentative route and segments. Each was 10 miles and a runner would cover the distance in 90 minutes. There would be 16 segments a day. There would be 5 teams of four runners. Each runner would run 10 miles a day for 4 days then get a rest day. Many people felt it was impossible. Dill having executed at that time three Olympic Torch Relays had the experience of having young adults pass out ice cold Coca-Cola while jogging with ski gear on for 84 days...he felt certain that with the right runners there would be no problem.

Next on Dill's list was to secure a sponsor. The strategy Dill came up with was to leave a BPR baton with every person he met and donate $25 to save a life on that person's behalf, and tell them he needed $10,000,000 to run around the world creating awareness for the safe drinking water issue. In the early Winter of 2005, Amanda Daniels and Dill were summoned to GolinHarris in Chicago to pitch the BP experiential marketing account. Dill did his usual high-energy pitch and at the end gave Amy Dick a BPR baton and told her the story. Two weeks later Amanda walks into Dill's office and informs him that BP loved our thinking, but was afraid of his high energy so they were going with GMR, a competitor.

In early Spring of 2006, the money from Coca-Cola ran out. Jin gets depressed and says all is lost. Dill says he is soldiering on, someone will come on board. Roughly thirty days later, Dill received a phone call from Amy Dick asking if it was ok for her to pitch BPR. GolinHarris was pitching for the entire Dow PR account and BPR was going to be the showcase. BOOM! They win the account and call Dill with the great news. We are running around the world. Suddenly, Jin is back on the team...it is amazing what money will do!

The planning begins in earnest to leave on 1 June 2007 at 10h00 EST from the UN in New York City and run the 40th parallel returning on 4 September 2007 at 10h00 EST. As fate would have it, during this time Jin decided that *ignition* was not fit to do the marketing portion of the BPR and he hired his next-door neighbor who put a new team in place. He cut *ignition's* fee by one million dollars! Dill tells the story of immediately falling on his hands and knees praying for new business so he can soldier on.

BOOM new business came...imagine BP used GMR for less than six months and gave the business to *ignition*.

The team left out on time on 1 June and arrived back 94 days later with Emmanuel Kibet arriving at the UN at exactly 10h00. There were guards there who said they witnessed a miracle. 1504 exchange points hit on time, one broken ankle, people who knew prayer works... thank you Max Helton.

Dill really learned a key lesson on BPR. The entire team should be "in" or the result will not be a success. Positive human energy did not really exist on BPR and it was a struggle. The team raised no real money for the foundation. On the last day in New York, GolinHarris and Dow thanked Dill for the challenging work and praised the execution which *ignition* did, but was not going to be a part of BPR going forward, and neither was Dill.

FISH MOBILE

It was the Fall of 2007 and John Stewart had an idea. He was going to put your church on your mobile telephone. Dill and John went to Nashville to visit with Thomas Nelson Publishing and share the idea. Thomas Nelson Publishing is one of the world's largest Christian book publishers. They presented Fish Mobile to an entire management team and to a person, they thought Dill and John were on to something big.

Next, Dill and John presented this "transformational church tool" to several of the mega church pastors and business people at a convention in Nashville. Again, a rousing success. The "pixie dust" was starting to be overwhelming, and Dill made the fatal mistake of falling in love with the idea and the team. He would learn the hard way that the church community is a tough crowd that the "not invented here syndrome" was alive and well.

Fish Mobile had three issues. First and foremost, it was ahead of its time. There were not enough smart phones on the same platform, so you had to write separate software for a myriad of devices. Second, the team could not create the compelling sales story that would land that first mega-church. Churches believed that it was going to be too time consuming for their staffs. When, it was easier than posting on Facebook. Thirdly, Dill under estimated the amount of focus it was going to take. He needed to be with the team sixty hours a week and at the time, he was still running *ignition*. In the end, Dill spent over $300,000 chasing an idea that he had fallen in love with.

At the time of this writing, John Stewart is working for the Boy Scouts of America as a top sales executive, Doug Boles is President of the Indianapolis Motor Speedway and Dill daily reads his soft leather Bible that he received in late October 2007 from Thomas Nelson! They all survived and thrived.

KOZMO.COM

The Summer of 1999 was a crazy time for Dill and Susan. They were married on 26 June, spent the next six weeks in Belgium to help The Coca-Cola Company solve and re-launch their entire portfolio of beverages, and in the Fall report to Germany. Just when it seemed it could not get busier an old friend calls Dill and says he and Susan need to be in NYC right away and meet Joseph Park. "Mr. Park had a big idea!", Chris Shimojima said with great enthusiasm. Kozmo.com had set up a warehouse in New York City in Manhattan and was delivering groceries, games, videos, magazines, books and music and the New York yuppies loved it. The idea was to have the service up and running in the top 20 markets ASAP. They wanted Dill and Susan's *ignition* to be the experiential marketing agency of record.

They accepted and immediately put Bill Fitzgerald on the account. Bill was quite a creative talent and before anyone knew what hit them, Bill had created three-foot tall metal "running man" ornaments to mount on the roofs of cars zipping around Manhattan. Within weeks, business was going great. The stories from the deliverymen and women were amazing as they were asked everything from walking people's dogs, to having sex!

As Dill was back in Belgium he was hearing of all the success, and he began to worry. When he was in New York, he had noticed that all with young employees were not using landlines but cell phones. This was the go-go dot.com world Dill was told. But he knew the telephone industry...landlines at the time were 5 cents a minute for long distance...the cell phone was up to 75 cents a minute. The business was expanding rapidly, and there were no controls. Not to mention, Joseph Park was an amazing fundraiser. He had raised a $250,000,000 war chest to go build Kozmo.com. He began to open new markets before he had proper processes in Manhattan ironed out. Kozmo.com became one of the poster children of the dot.com disaster. $250 million gone in under 36 months!

Dill watched a group of people fall in love with an idea, established no proper procedures, and wasted a lot of people's hard-earned cash. He preaches to anyone who will listen…Plan the work…Work the plan.

1999 COCA-COLA BELGIUM CRISIS

The morning of 23 June 1999, Dill hears that there is a severe problem going on in Belgium with Coca-Cola. He tells Susan that they will soon find out if they are on Coca-Cola's A-Team. That evening Dill and Susan got their answer, an email came to Dill from Tom Long, "where the hell are you, we have a problem in Belgium. Please call." On that call Tom explained that there had been a complete recall of all Coca-Cola beverages in Belgium, and Charlie Frenette, the CMO, was heading to Brussels to set up a war room and personally lead the re-launch. They wanted Dill and Susan there immediately. There was one slight problem. They were getting married on the 26th. They were married and on 27 June, flew to Brussels landing on the morning of 28 June and heading straight to Coca-Cola headquarters to begin the incredible job of re-launching the entire portfolio of beverages. It was 18 hours a day for the next 42 days. It was an honor to be on that team.

Charlie instructed Dill to get out into the country and talk to as many accounts and consumers as possible and each day at 17h00 Dill would report his learnings. There were several teams reporting in each evening, Advertising, Public Relations, Bottling, Distribution, and Dill's human touch. The first thing Dill would need was a taxi driver who spoke English and would work 18 hours a day. So, the first night after dinner Dill walked out to the taxi stand in front of the rail station and hollers "does anyone of you speak English?" A man in a beat-up Mercedes hollers "me Bathman I do." Dill mistakenly heard Batman and hollered back, "I am Robin", and a friend was made. These two crisscrossed Belgium for 42 days listening to the stories of customers and consumers. Dill was apologizing for the past and promising a bright new friendlier Coca-Cola in the very near future.

The 17h00 War Room meetings were difficult as Dill had to report the absolute truth with total POISE. Its customers or its consumers did not respect The Coca-Cola Company like it is accustomed to in most of the world. Their broken promises to retailers and a general arrogance that needed to be fixed were some of the issues at hand.

Dill reported the good news that the clear majority was ready to work with the Company to turn things around and to do it quickly. There are many detailed reports on what Coca-Cola did to win the day. Dill and Susan were fortunate to be part of working with the team on the experiential marketing programs. Dill had a young Coca-Cola executive from Belgium named Peter Schelstraete whom he worked with, they created a new refreshing humble Coke attitude in the streets. Dill and Peter along with several agencies trained thousands of Belgium youth to sample ice cold Cokes to the entire country and say we are sorry and thank you for your continued support in the future. As always Dill had a few tricks up his sleeves...he brought over a Gibson custom Contour Coca-Cola Bottle guitar, he built four Coca-Cola Harley-Davidsons, and the team created a game where you blind folded the contestant and had them reach into a large bucket and pull out the contour Coca-Cola bottle. They travelled the country making new friends and reacquainting themselves with their old ones. It was a magical Summer to be in Belgium. Someday, Dill will share some of the crazy stories with Batman at the wheel in the middle of the night racing back to Brussels from the opposite side of the country at 02h00!

Every night!

The wildest day was a Saturday in July 1999. It was the re-launch day. Dill and Charlie Frenette arose early to be at the biggest customer in the country to be there before opening. As Dill walked down the beverage isle, his worst nightmare stared him in the face. One-liter Coca-Cola bottles were leaking! Dill and Charlie quickly got the product off the floor and replaced with back up stock. Immediately Charlie says..." Dill get Susan and Batman...we need to get to the plant". Batman sped as if he was driving the Bat Mobile and upon arrival, the team found the plant closed...we were told it was running 24/7...it was not a good day for several people. The great news of the day was that there were no mishaps except the one Dill found before opening...Boom! Coca-Cola made friends and today they sell more product than pre-Crisis.

Dill always tells people the key learning in Belgium was quite simple, be humble, and always remember the customer is always right. As author David Salyers would say, Be Remarkable. Sort out how you are going to add value to everything you touch.

BEST OF THE 20TH CENTURY

Winter of 1997, Ben Higgs visits Dill at his Momentum office in Manhattan. Someone had told Ben that Dill was a big idea man and he had one. And it was. In two and one-half years, the end of the 20th Century was going to occur. Ben's idea was to have a global vote on The Best of the 20th Century. In every category you can imagine. Sports, movies, science, television, the arts, you get the picture the categories are endless. It was a big idea. Dill loved it and agreed to help and make it happen. In short, it was one of Dill's biggest disappointments as to this day he believes the idea should have been done…it was just ahead of it time.

What happened…Dill and Susan used their vast Rolodex to tee up meetings with some of the brightest marketers in the world. To a person, everyone loved the idea. What happened next was amazing. An A-Team was assembled to make The Best of the 20th Century come to life. Dickie Richardson owned the premier balloting company in the world. They handled the NBA, MLB, NFL and several other large all-star type balloted events, which entailed counting millions of ballots in a short amount of time. Neil Mulchay, salesman for Fox Television, became the champion sales person. He organized a group of meetings in January 1998 with the largest advertisers on the network. Susan gave presentation after presentation and each potential partner thought the idea was wonderful. The team truly believed they had a winner.

As Spring approached, the reality set in that the marketing world was not ready for such a large undertaking. The idea was not properly funded, and it became just that great idea that never saw the light of day.

Then on a sweltering day in June of 1998, a sheriff arrived at the door of *ignition*. He handed Dill an envelope containing a frivolous lawsuit. Ben Higgs was suing Rupert Murdoch, Dill and Susan Driscoll for $600,000,000. Susan about lost it, Dill said we did not steal his idea. Dill had been in the idea business for over 20 years at the time and he was known around the world for one thing, always telling the truth.

It took 18 months and $150,000 USD in legal fees, but they won. Ben Settled for $10,000 USD.

One important lesson here is if you truly believe in telling the truth 100% of the time then when someone tries to uncover some dirt on you, they will not find any. By being transparent in your business dealings, you will never have to worry about what is in that envelope that the Sheriff is handing you.

SALUTE OUR TROOPS

In Summer of 2010, Dill got a call from Joel Katz, an old friend and incredible lawyer, asking him to join him and several other senior entertainment industry executives to join the inaugural USO Entertainment Advisory Board. It was an honor for him to work with the team and the USO.

John Pray, the Executive Vice President of the USO at the time, headed up the Entertainment Advisory Board and called its first meeting in the Fall of 2010 in Los Angeles. During that first meeting Dill realized that his real value to the group would be to come up with ideas to raise money for the organization as it is not government funded as many people think. It was during a break that it hit Dill. He had a client named Kangaroo Express who had over 1600 stores in the Southeastern United States with many located near military bases. Dill asked himself the question...how much was a Coca-Cola... he thought bingo...you always get some change with coins. Then he thought how many transactions per day in these stores...and said to himself...if each store were to collect 10 dollars a day for the 100 days of Summer in 2011 it would raise $1,600,000 for the USO! Boom! Before he left Los Angeles he told the team that he would pitch the idea ASAP to Kangaroo Express.

Dill flies to Cary, North Carolina the following week to meet with John Fisher and Dave Henninger of Kangaroo Express. Dill and John had done some amazing projects together when John worked at Coca-Cola so John was always willing to hear a "crazy impossible idea to execute" from Dill. Dill pitched them on the idea of merchandising all 1600 stores with a theme of Salute Our Troops by rounding up your change. John and Dave thought the idea was big... and many of their stores were near military bases. They immediately said let's move on this, with one caveat...John Pray needed to attend the Kangaroo Express vendor meeting where we had to convince these vendors to pitch in and pay for the merchandising of all 1600 plus stores.

Dave set up the meeting at Duke in the Cameron Indoor Arena, the home of Duke Basketball...it was magic; a room full of the biggest consumer package goods companies in the world. Dill laid out the idea and introduced John Pray to tell his story while in the military and the needs of the USO...when he finished Rocky Stickman of Anheuser-Busch jumped out of his chair and told his story of being tied to a chair in the US Embassy in Tehran Iran in 1979 for 30 days. He was held hostage for 444 days! After these two speeches John asked for the money. Within 30 days, they had the $1.5 million they needed.

Next was the magical Summer of 2011. The team used Large Mouth Public Relations to come up with a PR plan, and Dill came up with the idea of putting a 1948 US Military Jeep on the road to visit stores with a video camera to let people visually Salute Our Troops. Dave and the team produced a website and with a PR plan two young University of Georgia recent graduates, Drew Snipe and Jim McGinn, hit the road to man the Jeep. The men toured the Southeast from Memorial Day to Labor Day filming consumers saluting Our Troops and putting their change in the can on the counter top. Everyone thought it would be a success if we raised $1 million...Dill said we needed to do $2 million. The final number was over $2.7 million!

Dill taught them to fish. Salute Our Troops raised over $10 million for military not-for-profits over the next four years. The key learning here is that the highest giving stores were in the poorest areas. To this day Dill claims the success was because when the right people do the right thing for the right reasons, God will provide.

CARRY THE LOAD

The first week of June 2011 Dill got a call from Jack Furst, a tremendous businessman whom he had met earlier in the year at a Boy Scout think tank. Jack asked Dill to fly ASAP to Dallas to meet a retired Navy Seal named Clint Bruce. Clint, Jack, and a couple hundred others had spent Memorial Day weekend walking around White Rock Lake for 20 hours and 11 minutes restoring the true meaning of Memorial Day and asking themselves "Who Are You Carrying". As Jack told Dill that day on the telephone Memorial Day to far too many Americans was a Mattress Sale or a Car Sale! Bingo! Dill told Jack of his idea to take Carry the Load on the road across America and hopped on the plane to Dallas to meet Jack and Clint.

Within the first hour of the meeting in Dallas Dill outlined how his team would map out four routes from across America each converging on Dallas on the Sunday of Memorial Day weekend and join the Dallas walk that would start at 15h38 on Sunday ending at 12h00 on Monday. Who else but Dill could pull this off they said. Dill said a lot of people could, but none with the passion of the team he will assemble. Jack asked who would be the executive Director of Carry the Load, and Clint immediately said Coleman Ruiz who was retiring from the Navy Seal team on 30 September 2011...Jack said done he would pay his salary himself.

Boom! 1 October 2011, Coleman arrived at Dill's office in Atlanta and the National Carry the Load Relay was born. The initial year the team only felt we could afford to do one route. Dill was all over it. Let's walk from West Point to Dallas. One-person at least walking five miles every two hours carrying the Carry the Load flag 24/7 for twenty-seven days. The route began at the Cemetery on the West Point campus to Robechan Park in Dallas, Texas. The route took the team south to NYC Ground Zero and Rescue Five, Philadelphia, Annapolis and the Naval Academy, DC and Arlington Cemetery, Charlottesville, and then they headed west to east Tennessee, Nashville, Memphis, Little Rock, Hot Springs, Texarkana and finally Dallas.

1 May 2012, Coleman, Dill, and Wes Conner stepped off from West Point. The team's support vehicle was an old Cruise America camper van. Everyday has a remarkable story which Dill will share on another day but suffice it say it was the hardest job he ever loved. Today Dill and his team are still taking the month of May off to walk from West Point to Dallas to "Restore the true meaning of Memorial Day" and ask the question "Who are you Carrying?"

The Carry the Load lessons are many, but the one to think about here is things are not always as they seem in business or in life. You are either carrying someone, someone is carrying you, or you are not in the game of life.

AT&T GOES NASCAR RACING

It is the Summer of 1998 and Dill gets a call from Chris Shimojima an old client from Nestle who is now working for AT&T. The telephone business was incredibly competitive at the time. You could "dial around" for long distance rates. With that as a backdrop, AT&T was launching The Lucky Dog Phone Company with their dial around number being 10.10.345. The first meeting was convened at "Death Star" (Dill's nickname for AT&T headquarters) in Basking Ridge, New Jersey. Howard McNally was the President, Chris Shimojima was the Brand Manager, and Brad Hobbs was the Assistant Brand Manager. This first meeting changed Dill and Susan's plans to keep *ignition* as a small consultancy. The Lucky Dog Team wanted to hire *ignition* to build a substantial experiential marketing platform for 10.10.345.

In the first meeting, the team mapped out a strategy to surprise and delight consumers in high traffic areas where the business was under performing. Dill hired ignitors who would wear backpacks that had the dial pad and a siren…when the person dialed down the middle 10.10.345 in under three seconds the siren and lights went off and they would receive a prize. The first test market was Atlanta, and the strategy worked; business picked up. The team was on to something.

The next strategy called for a national promotion to create a buzz and a call to action, AT&T needed people dialing down the middle! It was Fall of 1998 when The Lucky Dog Phone Company asked Dill to consider NASCAR which was experiencing tremendous growth at the time. Once again, the Rolodex was the key. Hal Price an old friend from Coca-Cola had left Coke to help build Jeff Gordon into a brand. Hal then introduced Dill to John Bickford who is Jeff's step-father and a very respected NASCAR insider. Dill and Susan go to Concord, North Carolina to meet with John and Hal. In that meeting Dill and Susan learned of the inner workings of team sponsorships and decided that they would approach it a bit differently. John suggested that the perfect team was Tyler Jet Motorsports. Tim

Beverly had just bought Darrel Waltrip's operation and was ready to "take NASCAR by storm". After months of negotiation, Dill got the call from Brad Hobbs, "let's go racing boys".

The crew chief was Phil Hammer with Rich Bickle at the wheel. Dill thought the world of both these guys and several other crew members including Chad Knauss who turned out well. Needless to say, the first few races were a struggle. The 10.10.345 car was caught up in a big crash in the Daytona 500 and the next week failed to qualify at Rockingham. Things on the track did not go well for the team, and Dill had to tell Phil Hammer he was out of a job when the car missed qualifying for Bristol by .001 of a second. The good news was the 10.10.345 NASCAR bus was a hit with the fans. In the middle of the season the Lucky Dog Phone Company's business model took a hit. 10.10.345 was 10 cents per minute and AT&T decided to lower its normal long-distance rate to 7 cents a minute. Boom! NASCAR was irrelevant. Dill had to have a pivot strategy, which he did.

10.10.345 still had the best rates to Mexico and Latin America and most Latinos love soccer. Dill went to the Rolodex and called his old friend Mike "Twig" McGlynn who ran the Lake Placid Soccer Center, one of the country's best. The two of them hatched a plan to rewrap the bus and sent it around the country giving soccer clinics. The star who travelled with Twig was Romerito, three-time FIFA South American player of the year. The clinics were an enormous success and the media loved Romerito. 10.10.345 hit the goal numbers and everyone was pleased except Tim Beverly the NASCAR owner.

Susan, Dill and Brad had negotiated with Tim the contract and according to many in NASCAR it was the first pay per performance by any major corporation. The deal was quite simple: a one-time $1 million check and a $100,000 check for qualifying each race, and a sliding scale from $100,000 for a win to $20,000 for a top twenty. If Tyler Jet had a terrific year, which we all hoped they would, the deal was a $10 to $11 million deal. As luck would have it, the year was tough on the racetrack and AT&T was not on the hook for $10 million. Dill and the entire AT&T/Lucky Dog team felt that NASCAR could be used as an effective marketing tool. They just saw the future a bit different than the rest of the NASCAR garage.

From 2000 to 2003, Dill and the team developed a strategy where they sponsored from 6 to 12 races a year with Andy Petree Racing and then BAM. The drivers were Mike Wallace, Kenny Wallace, and Ken Schrader. The brand was 1.800.CALL.ATT. It was quite a run. They enlisted Carrot Top a couple of seasons and had fans cheering 1.800.CALL.ATT to win prizes at the track. Dill has always felt this was one of his biggest successes as it took the rest of the NASCAR world 8 years to realize you did not need to sponsor an entire car for an entire season. Dill would tell you ATT would still be sponsoring a car if Nextel/Sprint did not shut them out!

EMBRAER PHENOM 100 AND PHENOM 300

It was the Spring of 2005 and Dill gets a call from David Allen who had a company that washed private jets at FBO's all over the world. Dill had met David at the Indy 500. He had a client that was getting ready to launch head first into private aviation. Embraer is a Brazilian manufacturer of passenger jets used by many airlines for their short hauls. Embraer was affectionately referred to as "jungle jets" due to their Brazilian heritage. A meeting is set in Atlanta for the following week.

In walks an executive from Embraer and the first thing you know he is asking Dill if experiential marketing will be an effective way to sell their new Phenom's. After all it sure was working for Dill's many clients over the years but the most expensive product Dill had ever marketed was a $70,000 automobile. The Phenom 100 was $2.5 million and the Phenom 300 was $5.7 million! He asked Dill who the target market was in the United States and how could he reach them. He also told Dill that the head of sales and marketing did not think experiential marketing was the way to go, he better have a great idea!

In a matter of two weeks, Dill found himself pitching what he will say is the hardest assignment of his life. Who is the customer...well... Dill explained the customer is the small to medium size business people who need flexibility in their travel, and it is the wealthy aviation buffs who always are looking for the newest toy. Where is the customer... how about the slopes of Aspen at Christmas...the polo fields of Palm Beach in March...the airfield at Oshkosh in July? What do we do... Dill explained to the team that if they delivered on their promise of the finest jets in their class his team would take a mock up, put it in a geodesic tent with great food and wine, and invite people to stop by after their day's activities were complete.

They all thought Dill was nuts, especially putting it on the slopes of Aspen, but were just intrigued enough to give him one test event. Once again Dill astounded them. The test event he wanted was the

Daytona 500. He bet his reputation on putting a "cool tent" right outside the driver/owner bus lot for the 2006 Speed Week. Remember Dill is a racer at heart and knew that many of the owners and drivers thrived on having the newest gizmo on the market...and they could afford one! Well guess what Dill was right. They sold six or seven that first week and eight years later they were still using experiential marketing to sell their jets. As he would say treat everyone the same and remember as Gussie Busch used to say...making friends is our business...especially when you are selling $3 to $6 million private airplanes!

BUTTERFINGER BB'S

It is a cold snowy day in January of 1992 and Dill is summoned by McCann Erickson to a meeting in White Plains. It was with Bob Sperry, Dennis O'Brien, and Chris Shimojima of Nestle. They had a new product and they needed a breakout idea to get Butterfinger BB's into 12 to 18-year-old consumers' hands then into their bellies. Time was of the essence as they wanted to be in market in 5 months. Dill asked for a couple of days to think.

Dill asked himself a couple of great questions...what never goes out of style...hard working, good looking guys and gals...what is an American icon that can deliver a bag of BB's...Frisbee...what is the hottest fad with kids in America at the time...Rollerblades...BOOM... teams of four...two girls...two guys...Test market was Buffalo. Picture yourself as a young teen the Summer of 1992 and you are at a concert and you see across the parking lot these young adults Rollerblading and tossing Frisbees out to your friends with a bag of BB's attached. Boom! They hit all the venues in Buffalo where their target was and they out-paced production.

What made this so important to Dill was that it proved to him and many others that experiential marketing or as Dill liked to call it" the human touch" really did have a place in the marketing mix.

Who would have ever thought, decades later, those same simple premises would still work in marketing.

COCA-COLA HARLEY'S / ICE ANGELS

It was the Fall of 1994 when Steve Hutcherson, the Brand Manager of Coca-Cola Classic, gave Dill a ring. He needed some thinking on how to reignite his brand with America's Blue-Collar Worker. Dill arrived in Steve's office ten days later with three ideas. One was a huge cement mixer painted like a Contour Coca-Cola bottle that would dispense ice cold Coke's down the cement chute. Everyone was thoroughly entertained, but the cement truck has yet to see the light of day. Dill has threatened in his retirement to build that truck. The second was the Coca-Cola Beverage Barge. Think pontoon boat with a fishing shack in the center with coolers full of ice cold Coca-Cola. The Barge spent weekends on high traffic lakes in the Southeast...think bass fishermen and free drinks...and during the week the Barge would be at Walmart parking lots having casting contests for the kids and free ice-cold Cokes. The Coca-Cola Beverage Barge became a fixture at FLW Bass Tour events and today the Barge resides in the pond in front of Dill and Susan's home in Osierfield, Georgia.

Finally, Dill brought out the idea which he says always works, an American icon delivering ice-cold Coca-Cola in the new contour bottle with hard working, good looking ignitors. Think Harley Davidson Road King with Coca-Cola Contour Bottle side car full of ice-cold Coke with a handsome rider and his sweetheart, one handing out product while the other making Polaroid's of the action. The crazy thing about this idea is it took them awhile to realize how big it was and how it would resonate with the blue-collar market. It was the week of May 1995 and Steve calls Dill and asks for the Harley to ambush the Pepsi Cola Fire Cracker 400 on 4th of July weekend. Dill hung up and yelled to Erik Petersen, "Red Alert! We need to locate 4 Road Kings and get Craftsman to start fabrication on the contour side cars...we are rolling to Daytona in seven-and-a-half-weeks with four Harley-Davidsons!" Everyone said Dill would not make the timeline; they did not realize the relationships he had created. A Harley Dealer outside Dallas had the bikes and he took American Express, Boom!

Like with Busch CitySki years earlier, God smiled on Dill and those Coca-Cola Contour Harley's. On Saturday 1 July 1995, Jeff Gordon driving 24 DuPont/Coca-Cola won the Pepsi 400! The Harleys were outside cruising the parking lots serving ice-cold Coca-Cola's in the new contour bottle to thousands of blue-collar race fans. In America the Coca-Cola Harley's are still used 20 years later. Dill always said the measure of a good idea to a great one is longevity. Funny how the 4th of July race is now sponsored by Coke Zero and Jeff is sponsored by Pepsi!

The rest of the story is in July of 1999 during the Belgium Crisis, Dill thought that the Belgian consumer would be fascinated to see a Coca-Cola Contour Bottle Harley Davidson pull up and sample ice-cold Cokes and make a Polaroid. That Summer, over 300,000 pictures were made on the bikes and over 300,000 ice-cold Cokes were sampled from the sidecars! The Harley's were becoming a huge hit and Dill was not done. Germany was next. David Haines and Rob Hindley were running the marketing at Coca-Cola Germany and asked Dill to come help them reintroduce brand Coke to the German market. One of the first things the team did the Fall of 1999 was to rebrand Coke Harleys as The Coca-Cola Ice Angels. Two teams of two bikes with their rider and their Angel toured Germany. They went everywhere you can imagine. Concerts, sporting events, bars, restaurants, even a 5-star hotel lobby! After year one 500,000 samples and over 500,000 Polaroids.

The lesson Dill was taught that Summer and Fall of 1999 was if you deliver your product to your consumer in a compelling way with hard working, good looking people; a great message; and ice-cold Coke, you will make friends. Friends who will look for you and best of all purchase your product. It is also critical to treat all your constituencies the same...with respect and dignity.

MEETBALL

It was early 2016 in Boston that Dill was introduced to a revolutionary innovative technology that he believes will transform the live event experience for consumers and sponsors. It is where the human touch intersects with the digital realm.

Ryan Owen and his brother Matt presented MeetBall to Dill on that fateful day.

Meetball provides the better live event experience by helping people efficiently navigate to people and places. Meetball provides the tools event hosts need to continue their events into the future with digital sponsorship opportunities, custom GPS maps, and the real-time communication tools that attendees demand. Conversion rates based on digital cues at events are 20-30 times higher than traditional means. Meetball provides a cost effective, scalable platform to achieve these goals and maximize opportunities around events.

This all sounds great but what does it mean? Imagine you are going to the Georgia versus Alabama Football game in Athens, Georgia with several of your friends. You are invited to three tailgates prior to kickoff and then an after party to be determined. How do you find all these people and places? Boom! You put the Meetball app on your phone and immediately a map of Athens pops up and locates your tailgates. And it can locate exactly where all six of your friends are. And to top off all those capabilities, you can communicate real-time with them all.

Dill has spent a lifetime producing some of the largest events in the world. The one common issue is always the same: getting sponsors and their consumers together. With Meetball problem solved... the Coca-Cola activation will pop up on Meetball and will guide the consumer to the exact location and provide a coupon on their phone for a free Coke with purchase.

Now sponsors can use Meetball to get their VIP's and consumers excited to visit their activities weeks before they attend the event. Think...Olympics...FIFA World Cup...US Open Golf...US Open Tennis...NASCAR...NFL...PGA...NBA...NHL...NCAA...Concerts... and the list goes on... A true game changer in how we can consume live events...coming at the perfect time as live attendance of events is slipping due to the comfort of the 72" television in the man cave!

After all this what is their positioning statement...let's start with a name change to Crowd Joy...

LIVE 8

2 July 2005 -- 11 Concerts -- 1,000 Artists -- 2,000,000 Spectators -- 3,000,000,000 Viewers -- 1 Message -- Nine Markets...London, Philadelphia, Paris, Berlin, Rome, Moscow, Chiba, Johannesburg, Barrie, Cornwall and Edinburgh.

20th Anniversary of Live Aid -- Team...Bob Geldof, Harvey Goldsmith, Kevin Wall, Susan and Dill Driscoll

Timing...Team pulled this off in 8 weeks from inception

Global Sponsor AOL

Most famous Artists...U2, Paul McCartney, Cold Play, Destiny's Child, The Who, Pink Floyd, Dave Matthews Band, Kieth Urban, Madonna, Elton John, Maroon Five, Robbie Williams, Kayne West, Sting, Jay-Z, Black Eyed Peas, Will Smith, Stevie Wonder, R.E.M., Duran Duran, Mariah Carey, Bonn Jovi, George Michael, Neil Young, Faith Hill, Tim McGraw, Toby Kieth, Alicia Keys, Shakira and many more.

ignition's role was to produce all the activation at each venue. Signage, back stage activities and front of house activations.
Fred Porro lead a team from London which spread out across the globe to make it happen. It was a crazy eight weeks of non-stop work. On the day before the event the executive producer Kevin Wall collapsed after the rehearsal.

The day of the show we kicked it off from London, and with the help of AOL, we lit up the world. AOL could not initially handle all the traffic. At the time it was the largest streaming event ever held.

There are too many side stories to tell...but one special one was Faye Dunaway wanting to get back stage in London and searching out Dill to get there. The ironic thing here was Faye worked in Saranac

Lake, NY (next town over from Lake Placid) before she was discovered and Dill used to go the Dew Drop Inn where she was a waitress and wish he had the guts to ask her out. That day he introduced her to Madonna and Bill Gates back stage in Hyde Park!

One last London story was Ricky Martin, not known in US at the time, but he stole the show. He Closed out Hyde Park and it was the most magical set Dill and Susan have ever witnessed. Over 80,000 fans singing from their hearts.

Message was heard Make Poverty History. Two days later in Edinburgh, the G8 met and relieved over a billion dollars of African debt.

The lesson here is with a mission that galvanizes the team, anything is possible. No one believed we could pull this off!

STAFFORD SCHOOL OF BUSINESS

It was 1 April 2012 and we had just closed on the sale of *ignition* to Havas. We went to Reed and Karen Miller's home in Lake Placid during mud season to spend three weeks contemplating our next move. We had a five year non-compete with *ignition* in place and Susan was adamant that we do not do a single thing to compromise our integrity. As we had been Entrepreneurs in Residence at UGA Terry School of Business for five years, we knew we loved helping students and we were good at it. The only real issue was Athens is 4 hours from the farm.

Upon arriving back to the farm in May, we reached out to Dr. David Bridges, the President of Abraham Baldwin Agriculture College (ABAC), to see what we might do to help students in South Georgia. We set up a meeting and it changed our lives. Dr. Bridges explained that a perfect storm had just occurred. The Dean of the Business School had retired and he needed a Dean. Susan would be interested if we could be co-Dean's and our black lab, Campbell, could come with us to work every day since he was a daily presence at *ignition*. In five weeks we moved into the Dean's office in Conger Hall and began creating a vision for the school. First, we felt we needed to name the school. As it turned out so did Dr. Bridges and the long-time benefactors of ABAC, the Stafford Family, was the perfect fit. We moved into Lewis Hall in the just renovated front of campus that Spring and the school was named The Stafford School of Business.

Next, we created Stafford Hall -- a community of students living on a wing of the on-campus dorms. Each student received a $500 room allowance each semester and the Team created activities for the students. The most important being we committed to feed those without an opportunity for a great Thanksgiving meal in Tifton, GA by raising money to provide and distribute the meals. Five years later Stafford Hall is much smaller but a group of dedicated students continue The Manna Drop. In the Fall of 2016, they raised over $20,000! That feeds a lot of people.

While all this was going on Susan worked with our amazing faculty and rewrote the business degree curriculum and pushed it through the system in record time. We had a four-year degree in Business and Economic Development focused on training young people in South Georgia to be successful small business owners.

We were also able to create an International Study Program that sent students to Vietnam and in year two across Europe stopping at Coca-Cola Country headquarters learning the nuisances of selling Coca-Cola products in diverse cultures.

We also taught hundreds of students Marketing, Family Business and a Seminar class on being Intrepid Spirits to meet the shadowy future without fear and conquer the unknown.

The lesson here is to set a vision and keep after it...even in face of bureaucracy which can make certain the best ideas may never see the light of day.

HIGHLIGHTS OF EXPERIENCES THROUGH THE YEARS - BIG EVENTS AND WHEN NEW CLIENTS CAME INTO OUR LIVES

2017
World Organization of the Scouting Movement, Surterra Texas License, Carry the Load, iScribe Board

2016
Surterra, Anchor Media, Carry the Load, Stafford School of Business, UGA Athletics, Rio Olympic Torch Relay, Take Charge, Meetball

2015
Surterra Florida License, Stafford School of Business, Carry the Load, Meetball

2014
Surterra Holdings, Stafford School of Business, FIFA World, Cup Trophy Tour, Sochi Olympics Torch Relay, Sochi Olympics Coca-Cola Host City Activation, Carry the Load

2013
Stafford School of Business, Carry the Load, USO Executive Advisory Board

2012
London Olympic Torch Relay, London Olympics Coca-Cola, Boom Box, Entrepreneur in Residence Terry College of Business University of Georgia, Stafford School of Business, Carry the Load, Salute Our Troops, USO Entertainment, Advisory Board, Sold *ignition* to Havas, Gameball Relay - UGA Shepard Center, Sprite NBA Street Teams, BP Olympic Activation, Coca-Cola Davos

2011

Entrepreneur in Residence Terry College of Business University of Georgia, USO Executive Advisory Board, Salute our Troops, Coca-Cola 125th Anniversary Concert, Delta 70th Anniversary, Girl UP, UN Foundation, Kelloggs Gameday, BP Surprise & Delight, Victoria's Secret

2010

Entrepreneur in Residence Terry College of Business University of Georgia, Vancouver Olympic Torch Relay, Vancouver Olympics Happiness House, FIFA World Cup Trophy Tour, Chick-fil-A, Coca-Cola Special Olympics Soccer, Match on World Cup Pitch in Jo'Burg, Dow Live Earth Relay, Nothing but Nets, Aircell/GOGO

2009

Entrepreneur in Residence Terry College of Business University of Georgia, Dow Live Earth, Digital College Network, Embraer, Grand Am, X Games, Coca-Cola Live Positively, BP Mazda Show Car, Blackberry, SunTrust

2008

Beijing Olympic Torch Relay, Atlanta Motorsports Park, Brand Atlanta, Bill & Melinda Gates Foundation, Kia, UN Foundation, Delta Air Lines Sundance, Coca-Cola Training for Perfect Serve China, Cheerios

2007

Blue Planet Run, Live Earth, American Express, BP, CARE, CNBC, F1, Microsoft, Williams F1, Delphi, Nike, Abu Dhabi F1 Street Course, Chivas Regal, Cirque Du Soleil, Pirelli

2006

FIFA World Cup Trophy Tour, Torino Olympic Torch Relay, Earthlink, Intel, Levis, MasterCard, Panther Racing (IRL), NCAA Final Four, John Deere, Motorola, Honda Civic Black, Eyed Peas Tour, Coke Blak, TAB Energy, Nokia New Years Eve (global), Toshiba, Vodafone F1, F1 Awards Banquet

2005

Live 8, British Telecom, ESPN, General Motors, Intel, McDonald's, Song, UK Music Hall of Fame, Warner Brothers, General Lee Dukes of Hazard Tour (Dill Driscol, yes one l, is Billy's Crew Chief in the movie), Coca-Cola Zero, Slim Jim, AOL Live 8, Nokia Live 8

2004

Athens Global Olympic Torch Relay, Athens Olympic Torch, Relay (Greece), Burger King, Disney, Firestone, Pioneer, Delta Air Lines Mini Coopers, Camp EBay, Vodafone Cricket, Vodafone F1

2003

AOL, Delta Air Lines, Indy Racing League, Coca-Cola Step With It (all middle schools in America), Coca-Cola Slim Can, Burger King 4th of July Great American Hamburger, Give Away, AT&T NBA, AT&T X Games, Sprite Liquid Mixx Tour, AT&T NASCAR Carrot Top

2002

Salt Lake City Olympic Torch Relay, Harley Davidson, Nestea, Vodafone Heathrow Pop Up Store, Coca-Cola Real Thing on Main (SLC), AT&T College, Coca-Cola Real Music, Vodafone F1 Ferrari, Fanta Fantanas, AJ Foyt Racing

2001

Channel One/CDC, CNN/Turner, MSN/Microsoft, Coca-Cola 7 Eleven, Diet Coke with Lemon Vespa, AT&T NASCAR, Ultimate TV

2000

Sydney Olympics Coca-Cola Kids Program, E Trade, AT&T NASCAR, Coca-Cola Germany, Kozmo.com, EZ Gov.com

1999

Coca-Cola Belgium Crisis, 10-10-345 NASCAR (AT&T), 10-10-345 Soccer (AT&T), The Event Department (Germany), COPA America Paraguay, Discovery Channel, Kellogg's, Coca-Cola Austria

1998

Founded *ignition*/ McWhorter Driscoll, FIFA World Cup Trophy Tour, Lucky Dog Phone Company (AT&T), Nagano Olympic Torch Relay, Wham-O Summer Invasion, Rubbermaid, The Coca-Cola Company, Coca-Cola North America, Sprite Program South Africa, Concert at Pyramids for Mubarak

1997

Republic of South Africa Coca-Cola Relaunch, Caught Red Handed Coca-Cola South Africa

1996

Atlanta Olympic Torch Relay, Coca-Cola Olympic City, AT&T Pavilion Centennial Olympic Park, Coca-Cola Christmas Caravan, Outback Madden Cruiser

1995

Coca-Cola Harleys, Nestea Boston Tea Party, Coca-Cola Caught Red Handed North America, O'Doul's Relaunch PGA/NASCAR, SportsLab, Carolina Panthers Gameball Relay

1994

Cherry Coke Sonic Shuttle, Rockola Coca-Cola Mexico, Nescafe Mocha Coolers, SportsLab Fund Raising, Coca-Cola Contour Bottle Commercialized throughout the US

1993

Founded Momentum, Drive America Quality, OK Soda, Coca-Cola Blockbuster Movie Critic, Coca-Cola Contour Bottle Project Begins

1992

Sports Illustrated Sports Fest, GM Credit Card, TAB Clear

1991

Budweiser Superfest, Budweiser Heuy Lewis and the News Tour, Nintendo Campus Challenge Presented By Geo

1990
GoGo My Walkin' Pup, Budweiser Rolling Stones Urban, Jungle Tour, Butterfingers BB's, Spring Breakout Six Flags, Cadillac Classic Skins Game, GM Top Gun TV Ad, Creative Trips to Germany

1989
NARB (National Association of Record Breakers), Budweiser Steel Wheels Tour, Good Humor Truck Tour, Michelob Light Tour Challenge, Spuds MacKenzie, Cadillac Classic Skins Game, Creative Trips to Mexico

1988
Sold World Sports Promotions to McCann, Busch CitySki, Michelob Light City Beach, Pepsi Challenge, Kellogg's Mini Wheats, Scouting for U Natural

1987
Busch CitySki, Michelob Light Town Challenge, Michelob Light City Beach, Natural Light City Fish

1986
Busch CitySki US 12 cities, Busch CitySki London, Michelob Light City Beach

1985
Busch CitySki 9 cities, Moved Headquarters to Aspan

1984
Founded World Sports Promotions, NASCOM, Busch CitySki Boston

1983
...via World Wide Ski Corporation, Miller Lite NASTAR, Michelob Light Tour Challenge, Pepsi NASTAR, Appleton Rum Runs, NASTAR Guide

1982
...via World Wide Ski Corporation, Miller Lite NASCAR, Pepsi NASCAR, Michelob Light Town Challenge, NASTAR Guide

1981
Schlitz NASTAR, Pepsi NASTAR, NASTAR Guide

1980
Carroll Reed Ski Shops - Buyer/Manager

1979
Carroll Reed Ski Shops - Buyer/Manager, Rossignol Television Advertising Program

1978
Bloomingdale's NYC - Buyer Plaza Two Coats

1977
Equipe Sports, Campbell Soup Indian Tank Sampling Program

1976
Equipe Sports Founded, Nike Waffle Trainer - indoor retail running track

1975
Teacher/Coach Northwood School, Soccer/Skiing/Lacrosse, Economics/Humanities

1974
Teacher/Coach Northwood School

...any many many more. Over the years, the memory fades and all cannot be remembered, but the fun, challenging and learning experiences just never go away. As Dill and Susan say, "There are no new ideas, just old ideas filtered through a new screen."

Experiential Marketing was not recently created as some like to claim. Think Moses going up the Mountain, talking to God, getting the tablets, starting the movement that continues for years to come. May we all engage in many more experiences in our lifetimes!

Made in the USA
Middletown, DE
11 September 2018